YOU CAN'T MARKET MANURE AT LUNCHTIME

YOU CAN'T MARKET MANURE AT LUNCHTIME

AND OTHER LESSONS FROM THE FOOD INDUSTRY FOR CREATING A MORE SUSTAINABLE COMPANY

MAISIE GANZLER

HARVARD BUSINESS REVIEW PRESS
BOSTON, MASSACHUSETTS

Library of Congress Cataloging-in-Publication Data

Names: Ganzler, Maisie, author.
Title: You can't market manure at lunchtime : and other lessons from the food industry for creating a more sustainable company / Maisie Ganzler.
Description: Boston, Massachusetts : Harvard Business Review Press, [2023] | Includes index.
Identifiers: LCCN 2023046069 (print) | LCCN 2023046070 (ebook) | ISBN 9781647825676 (hardcover) | ISBN 9781647825683 (epub)
Subjects: LCSH: Farm produce—Marketing. | Food industry and trade. | Sustainable development.
Classification: LCC HD9000.5 .G26 2023 (print) | LCC HD9000.5 (ebook) | DDC 338.1/90688—dc23/eng/20231227
LC record available at https://lccn.loc.gov/2023046069
LC ebook record available at https://lccn.loc.gov/2023046070

ISBN: 978-1-64782-567-6
eISBN: 978-1-64782-568-3

For Winnie Larsen
We have so much left to discuss.

Contents

Interviews

YOU CAN'T MARKET MANURE AT LUNCHTIME

Introduction

"You spray the shit in the air! People can't breathe!" Fedele Bauccio, CEO of Bon Appétit Management Company—and my boss—is fired up. He's talking to the chief sustainability officer of America's largest pork producer, who has flown to our Palo Alto offices to ask why Fedele keeps publicly bad-mouthing them, especially since we buy a lot of pork from his company. Well, Fedele is telling him.

Fedele's main bone to pick with this boss of hogs is the poor air quality in the communities surrounding the company's farms. An industrial swine operation can generate as much waste as a medium-sized city. Thousands of pigs are kept in barns with slatted floors, so when they do their thing, the waste falls through the openings. The pig poop is collected in large pits called manure lagoons, piped out, and sprayed onto nearby fields. Imagine liquid that smells like rotten eggs raining down from the sky—that's how these industrial pork farms deal with waste.

Fedele is on a roll. He's incredibly passionate about these manure lagoons. Before this face-off between two forces in the food industry, he spent two years on the Pew Commission on Industrial Farm Animal Production. It brought him to North Carolina to see, and smell, this issue firsthand, and it left an indelible mark on him (literally, he threw away the clothes he wore because he couldn't get rid of the odor). He'd looked out on a lake of manure and watched as its contents were shot into the air. He'd sat in the living rooms of the families whose homes were near the farms—communities with sky-high rates of asthma and cancer—who couldn't let their children play outside because the stench was giving them respiratory problems.

Those experiences changed him. So, whenever asked, and sometimes even before he is asked, Fedele rails against factory farming in general, and the pork operations he saw specifically. He even names names, including that of our very own contracted supplier. As you can imagine, they aren't too happy about that. Thus, here we are, in a pristine conference room thousands of miles away from the farms in question, as he yells about raining manure.

I wholeheartedly share Fedele's outrage, and it's my job to leverage this moment to make change for those families and those pigs—and to get my company credit for doing so. As Fedele continues to harp on fecal matter, however, all I can think about is how hard this task will be because of how incredibly unappetizing the topic is. There is just no way to talk to your customers about taking action on pits of poop while they're enjoying their lunch, or even after they've eaten. Can you imagine sitting down to dine underneath a poster about manure? What's the headline? "The shit created by your pork sandwich was safely handled?" That's not going to sell more BLTs.

That's, of course, where the unusual title of this book comes from— it's become something of a mantra for me, and a story I use often to talk about the challenges you're here to address. But the title also represents, figuratively, the greater struggle *all companies* face with sustainability. The truth is, consumers, and other stakeholders of yours, truly don't want to think about this stuff *at all*, and when I say "this stuff," I might as well be talking about sustainability in general. I don't mean they don't care—many, many do. But when I get into the details, the complexities, the hard choices, the poop, even the most ardent supporter can lose the will to make the necessary change.

The trick for a for-profit business trying to build a more sustainable system, then, is to gain a market advantage by doing good, environmentally or socially, and then get credit for doing so with an audience with a short attention span. You can't market manure at lunchtime, no, but you can't let that stop you from figuring out how to move forward more sustainably.

This effort must start with defining *sustainability*, a term I've already used six times but for which, as you might imagine, there are many interpretations. Once, while at a Sustainable Food Lab event, I was chatting with a large-scale soybean farmer. He mused, "I've taken as much of the labor out of my business as possible. I just don't see how I can make it any more sustainable." Hmm, I thought, no mention of the chemicals he's using, no worry about genetically modified seeds. We're not talking about the same thing when we say "sustainable."

Sustainability has become a buzzword in marketing everything from food to clothing, from tourism to buildings. When it entered the common business lexicon, I heard two definitions applied more than others (though I heard many). The first was "Meet[ing] the needs of the present without compromising the ability of future generations to meet their own needs," a definition based on *Our Common Future*, a 1987 UN World Commission on Environment and Development report.[1] The second was "In our every deliberation, we must consider the impact of our decisions on the next seven generations," from the founding document of the Iroquois Confederacy.[2]

Both of those are beautiful sentiments, but neither is adequate if you're trying to write a purchasing policy for chicken.

At my company, Bon Appétit, we were guilty for years of being just as poetic and vague. We used the tagline "Food service for a sustainable future" without being clear on exactly what our vision for that future was. When giving talks, I would fall back on one of the two broad definitions above and then make a joke about sustainable business being like pornography; you know it when you see it. That flippancy didn't belie the depth of our commitment or the authenticity of our claims. Not having a solid definition of sustainability both hampered me in differentiating Bon Appétit from its competitors who were also making loose claims, and it opened us up to accusations of greenwashing because of the breadth of the promise.

I called on our employees across the country to help us define "sustainable food service." We crowdsourced a description that captured the values of our team and the issues most relevant to our business:

> Flavorful food that's healthy and economically viable for all, produced through practices that respect farmers, workers, and animals; nourish the community; and replenish our shared natural resources for future generations.

Now we had something I could test purchasing policies against, and we could communicate to the world in one not-so-short sentence what we cared about.

You should craft a similar definition for your business. The more specific, the better. In some cases, industry groups have done this work for their sector. When talking about sustainable tourism, the World Tourism Organization refers "to the environmental, economic and socio-cultural aspects of tourism development, and a suitable balance must be established between these three dimensions to guarantee its long-term sustainability."[3] Not bad, but maybe, if you're running an eco-resort in Costa Rica, you want to get even more specific and call out rainforest preservation and the economic security of the Bribri people.

Before using the lessons in this book to craft your policies and build sustainability into your brand, I urge you to take the time to do your own *Mad Libs* exercise to define a sustainable future as you see it. Having a clear vision will help you in every step I outline in the coming chapters, from picking your issues to telling your story.

. . .

Consumers and critics often think that sustainability is a switch somewhere that corporate executives can flip and simply pay the farmer more for regenerative agricultural practices, the factory owner a bonus to use only ethical recruiters of migrant workers, or a premium to the mining company to ensure you get conflict-free minerals. That a company could be more sustainable if it would just spend more for its inputs.

I've learned from experience that the complexities of national and even global supply chains, competing priorities, and the challenge of messaging make authentically greening a company much harder than simply writing a bigger check. Through my successes and failures leading an almost $2 billion corporation toward a more sustainable future, I've come to understand that there are, instead, dozens of small switches you need to flip daily.

As chief strategy and brand officer of Bon Appétit Management Company, I am the architect of this award-winning food-service company's groundbreaking approach to responsible purchasing and a leading force behind the food industry's pivotal shift toward sustainability. I have traveled to what seemed like the end of the earth to build a brand based on sustainability. On my quest to understand the complex certification schemes of the aquaculture industry, I followed shrimp from ponds in the Mekong Delta to a factory with hundreds of Vietnamese women leaning over conveyor belts to remove the crustaceans' heads, shells, and digestive tracts by hand. I've walked across the border from Yuma, Arizona, to Mexicali, Mexico, to interview farm leadership teams formed to create a more equitable food system. I slept on a church floor after marching through South Florida protesting the treatment of farmworkers in the tomato fields. I've spent countless hours in meetings in windowless conference rooms in airport hotels.

The hardest part of all this? Boiling these experiences down into actionable purchasing policies and pithy marketing campaigns.

I did eventually stick the seemingly impossible landing on the manure thing: I improved our pork supply chain and, by doing so, built brand recognition for Bon Appétit as an industry leader in the sustainable food industry. It took over *a decade* of work, a series of small wins and big setbacks, and—spoiler alert—our marketing materials never mentioned manure lagoons.

This is how I made Bon Appétit Management Company the gold standard for sustainability, with recognition from prestigious organizations like the James Beard Foundation. This is how I helped to grow the company to more than $1.7 billion in revenue. This is the business of sustainable food.

In this book, I've distilled almost thirty years spent proving that planetary and personal health can thrive alongside profit into five lessons for building a business and a brand on sustainability:

Learn how to pick your battles

Learn how to make sustainability your mission (literally)

Learn how to make meaningful change

Learn how to fix things when you fall short

Learn how to tell your story

These lessons are designed to benefit any company integrating sustainability into their fundamental way of doing business. Even if you're concerned with cotton farms instead of pig farms, factory workers rather than farmworkers, or e-waste rather than chicken waste, you will get a road map for where to start, what proverbial manure lagoons might lie in your path, and how to make "making the world a better place" more than a platitude. You can apply these lessons in any business, whether your primary sustainability challenge is overseas shipping or consumer packaging. It doesn't matter. My stories will focus on the industrial food system, but you can mine them for the techniques and ideas that apply to your business. It's the behaviors and the practices that will lead you to a more sustainable future.

Read these five lessons in order or skip around. Together, they're a manual for joining corporate social responsibility with fiscal responsibility. "Lesson One: How to Pick Your Battles" will help you gather, organize, and evaluate myriad issues your company could take on. (Pro tip: there will be more you *can* do than you *should* do.) "Lesson Two: How to Make Sustainability Your Mission (Literally)" will inspire you to think through how your company's overarching goals are supporting or hampering your sustainability efforts. In "Lesson Three: How to Make Meaningful Change," you'll find leverage points for making change and setting parameters and targets to measure against, moving sustainability from vague promises to real, operational effectiveness. Things won't always go as expected, so "Lesson Four: How to Fix It When You Fall Short" helps you steer clear of greenwashing, which is focusing on the appearance of being sustainable rather than doing the work of actually operating sustainably. Finally, in "Lesson Five: How to Tell Your Story," you'll learn how to craft effective messages about complicated scientific topics and spread the word about your efforts (without making your customers lose their lunch), because getting credit matters and is an intrinsic part of building a sustainable business.

Along the way, you'll hear honest tales from a dozen top executives about how they faced their own "porks" in the road, like how Jim Perdue decided to welcome animal activists into the barns of his eponymous chicken company, how Gary Hirshberg sees political action as his secret marketing weapon—even though it got Stonyfield Organic yogurt banned from the café in the US Capitol Building, and what Walter Robb remembers as the most divisive issue for Whole Foods Market's executive team. These industry legends expand the lessons beyond my experience, with expertise spanning everything from consumer packaged goods to fresh fruit production, from fast casual restaurants to fine dining, and from stocking animal barns to stocking grocery shelves.

This book is packed full of stories and real-life examples from the food world, but I want to stress that the lessons are universal. I'm confident you'll recognize yourself and your own challenges, and hopefully laugh along the way, as you learn how to put these practices into action at your food company, clothing line, manufacturing business, or widget production house. This isn't an academic exercise; this is concrete guidance you can use starting tomorrow. My experiences will save you a trip around the world . . . or maybe inspire you to take one.

You can't market manure at lunchtime, but you can change the world—and make money while you're at it.

How to Pick Your Battles

"Please leave all your clothing behind the yellow line, enter the shower, wash with soap, and shampoo your hair. Exit the shower out the other side, and you'll find clean underwear, a bra, coveralls, and socks waiting for you."

Wait, what? I have to take off all my clothes, take a shower, and then put on someone else's undies? Why, yes! And then do the same thing again in reverse after the tour. It's called "showering in" and "showering out." And what sort of facility requires this level of biosecurity? Am I seeing a nuclear plant? A sensitive scientific experiment? Nope, I'm going to see pigs. Yes, pigs. Those animals known for bathing in mud, whose enclosures have become (erroneously) synonymous with a mess. I'm going to a literal pigsty.

I was on the hunt for gestation-crate-free pork, to make Bon Appétit Management Company (we usually call it just Bon Appétit, or BAMCO) the first food-service company to meet this high bar for animal welfare. These clothing precautions were necessities when touring a sow-breeding facility run by the Clemens Food Group for its Farm Promise line of pork products, because, in addition to spending less time in gestation crates, Farm Promise pigs are never given antibiotics, so protecting these animals from disease is critical. They've been selectively bred to be the most efficient piglet producers possible, but those near-identical genetics make them vulnerable. Bring in foreign bacteria on my clothing, or apparently even my underwear, and I could introduce an illness that—without the ability to use antibiotics as medicine—could wipe out the entire herd.

That hunt, and the need for me to be in that shower stall putting on granny panties and a sports bra (I know you were wondering) provided by a potential new pork supplier, were necessary because that conversation I mentioned in the introduction with our manure-spewing vendor broke down. I have to say, it was brave of that corporate executive to come meet us—his critics—on our turf and open the lines of communication. The problem was the chasm between us was as wide as one of their hog factory's manure lagoons.

Fedele and I did wade in. We made a proposal: "Set up a little farm that raises hogs sustainably and we'll buy everything you can produce. We know we'll have to pay more, but that's OK. No nontherapeutic antibiotics. No inhumane practices like gestation crates and tail docking. No manure lagoons! We'll buy that pork."

Sounds good, right? Our small but mighty pork farm would solve environmental issues, antibiotic overuse, and animal cruelty in one fell swoop. Unfortunately, I learned it's impossible to take on that many issues at once. I knew a fair amount about the industrial food system, but that conversation began my true education and kicked off battles on too many fronts.

Battle number one: How do we measure "sustainable" hog production? We needed a credible third-party standard. Since Fedele was so focused on the manure lagoons, I suggested the Food Alliance certification, because it's the only standard that covers animal welfare as well as the environment.

Battle number two: What do we do with the rest of the pig? Turns out Bon Appétit chefs use a lot of bacon, a fair amount of ham, and not that many chops or shoulders. I knew bacon came from the belly, but I didn't know that a typical 250-pound hog yields just 8 pounds of bacon—if you're lucky. I also didn't know that you can get twice as much ham as center-cut pork chops (two legs versus one loin), but if you want tenderloin, you can't also have pork chops. Well, I learned. We'd never buy enough baby back ribs to cover all the bacon we go through. So, we needed a partner: another purchaser that wanted the parts of the pig that we didn't want. One that wouldn't be too price sensitive. We immediately thought of Whole Foods.

Whoops, that took us back to battle number one: standards. Whole Foods requires its meat to be Global Animal Partnership (GAP) certified. GAP is a great animal welfare standard, but it doesn't cover the environmental aspects of pork production. That left those darn manure lagoons in place. Were we going to ask the pork producers to comply with two standards? This stumbling block kept us from talking to Walter Robb, then co-CEO of Whole Foods, about pork, but I did speak to him recently. (Read my interview on page 127.)

Battle number three: the economics of production. Suddenly, I had to think about the number of sows on a farm and piglet mortality rates; how to be sure we receive our "special" humanely raised pork, the producer will have to segregate our pork from all its other pork throughout its supply chain. That meant sending "our" hogs through the slaughterhouse separately. Now we're talking slaughter line rates and processing facility capacity. It got to be a lot of pigs really quickly. Even though we were offering to pay more per pound, our little utopian farm wasn't economically viable for this big producer to create. Our $7.5 million in annual pork purchases couldn't guarantee enough volume to make that imaginary farm work.

Notice how something that seems simple at the start—let's buy responsibly raised pork—becomes a labyrinth of complex interdependencies and difficult decisions and how simple economics often squelch good ideas. Even if it wasn't complicated to achieve our goal (and it was), it wasn't a viable business. This is what you'll face when you start doing this right. You'll be learning all the time, you'll face situations that seem hopelessly complex, and you'll feel like you're losing the battles you take on. That might just mean you haven't picked the right issues.

Battle-weary myself, I proposed another approach to the pork dilemma. We take on the most egregious practices first. Maybe we can't solve all the problems, but can we at least get the sows out of gestation crates?

In the pork industry, most breeding sows are confined to cages or gestation crates roughly the same size as they are, 24-7, during their entire four-month pregnancy. They can't even turn around. They are then placed into a slightly larger farrowing crate to give birth and suckle piglets for a few weeks before being re-impregnated and put back into a gestation crate. Horrible!

I drew a line in the mud. Within five years, we would phase out all pork from animals raised using gestation crates. We'd be the first food-service company to take a stand on the treatment of hogs. We'd publicly call out this inhumane practice and shame the producers into making change.

I'd picked my battle. I was going to need a new pork supplier and a pair of clean underwear.

The ultimate goal when creating a brand based on sustainability is to make meaningful change *and* have people recognize your effort, which can create a virtuous circle. The perfect initiative creates a real environmental or social effect, sets a high bar to which peer companies must rise if they want to stay competitive (thus multiplying your impact), and lands your brand on the front page of the *Wall Street Journal*. This all starts with picking the right battle—deciding which issues you are going to take on.

Some battles will do good for the world but won't gain you a competitive advantage as a business. Others will make you look good but do little for true sustainability. You need to find the ones that do real good and help raise your profile. You must be strategic in your approach. Think through all your stakeholders, identify the right battles for your business, and you'll disrupt the system, earn positive brand association, and set yourself apart in the market.

Sometimes the battle finds you. At other times, you're going to have to proactively look for ideas and decide between several possible directions, because unfortunately there are seemingly endless ills your company could take on.

I'm constantly asking myself, "What's the next magic?" What's the next issue that's going to propel our company forward by making change in the world and setting us apart in the minds of our customers, the industry, and the media? Jumping into battle without answering this question will create a lot of disparate items on your to-do list that don't add up to a cohesive idea or brand. Your efforts will diffuse and you'll be less likely to make a big impact.

One of the first things Roma McCaig did when she joined Clif Bar & Company as senior vice president of impact and communications was to help them narrow their battle plans. As she told me, "At Clif, there was no shortage of aspiration. They wanted to do everything! We would joke about how at Clif they were excellent at focusing on a bunch of littles. It was 'We want to change the world through every little action we could possibly take.' Clif just isn't big enough to be that agent of change. I helped them get focused. 'Of all these things, where can we actually make a difference? What makes sense for us as Clif?'" This is just another way of asking, what is the next magic? (Read more about Roma's experiences picking battles at Clif and elsewhere on page 88.)

While admirable, Clif was typical of what I see with many well-meaning companies that are passionate about becoming more sustainable: they were fighting too many battles, and the battles were too big. They had yet to identify their main issue—the one that customers could easily connect with and eventually associate directly with their brand—or a coherent narrative that would give meaning to their list of initiatives. There was a lot of time, effort, and money spent, but they hadn't created magic. A long list of sustainability efforts reads to customers more like their roommate's chore chart than a path toward bettering the company and the world.

So, to pick the right battle, you want to break it down to three steps:

Step one: Find your focus. Decide if you'll be single-minded or take on multiple issues.

Step two: Identify ideas for new initiatives by following your passion, talking to advocates, and listening to customers.

Step three: Manage your portfolio of ideas so you can take on the right battles at the right time.

Let's take each in turn.

Step One: Find Your Focus

If you want to build a brand based on sustainability, rather than quietly do good in the world, find a focus that all your stakeholders, employees, customers, and the press can quickly understand. That can be a single issue or a set of issues that you group together in a logical way. Do you want to go deep in one area like climate change, animal welfare, or packaging and try to own that issue, or do you want to address a wide range of topics so that you're known as the all-around sustainability champion? Answer that question before you act. Your response will determine if you should adopt a single-minded or multipronged strategy.

When to Be Single-Minded

For some brands, the issues they take on are their raison d'être, their reason for being. This is a single-minded approach. Entire companies have been built on one issue, such as child labor (Tony's Chocolonely), the scarcity of clean drinking water (RightWater), and the loss of biodiversity (Row 7 Seed Company).

For many years, such social ventures were seen as niche startups. That's changed with the rise in purchasing power of socially conscious millennials and Gen Z, and as people lose faith in traditional institutions' ability to make positive social and environmental change. Corporations are seen as even more powerful than governments. More and more people are starting businesses, *big* businesses, with the express purpose of making a difference in the world.

Pat Brown, the founder of Impossible Foods, is a perfect example of this shift. Pat left Stanford University after years as a professor of climate science, deciding the most impactful thing he could do to stem global warming was not to continue lecturing but to move people away from eating beef to enjoying plant-based alternatives. The company's founding purpose isn't to create wealth (though of course it must promise to make a lot of money for investors to garner the $2.1 billion it's raised) or to promote animal welfare, which it may do as well. Its mission is to "make the global food system truly sustainable by eliminating the need to make food from animals."[1] Impossible Foods literally had a section on its website called "Why We Exist." After detailing the scary facts about climate change in big, bold, all-caps letters, it said . . .

THE BEST, FASTEST SOLUTION TO ACCELERATING THESE CLIMATE ACTION GOALS? REDUCE RELIANCE ON ANIMALS TO MAKE MEAT.

No one at Impossible Foods is wondering what issues to pick. It's crystal clear in the company's single-minded DNA.

If you tackle a single subject, it's got to be unique enough to create differentiation or it won't lead to market advantage. For example, in many categories today, Certified Organic is no longer unique. A quick Amazon search for "organic crackers" yields over four thousand results. With so many brands addressing the same issue, the organic label alone will not persuade someone to buy your product over a competitor's.

One way to think about which issue will create differentiation is to think about the surprising case. What feature would be least expected for your product? Consider organic again. Amy's Drive Thru, a small restaurant chain in Northern California, brings organic to where it's least expected—fast food. By pairing organic with vegetarianism and convenience, Amy's has created a brand that is truly different from its competitors and having a drive-through separates Amy's from other health-focused restaurants.

When a company is built around a single-minded purpose, it's critical to the authenticity of the brand that you as the brand holder understand the issue deeply and that everything you do is aligned with your mission. You are going to be held to the highest standard when it comes to that issue.

When to Take a Multipronged Approach

Corporations are seen as having the ability to solve a whole host of global challenges when it comes to sustainability. Deciding which issue to address to create a strong brand is a less obvious choice when you're trying to build a generally sustainable company—meaning when your core reason for existing is to sell a product or service, but you also want to do it in an overall responsible way. I suspect most of you reading this book will fall into this category.

If so, you need to take a multipronged approach to picking your battles. Select a series of issues that cover a range of topics, make change in several ways, and communicate that you are broadly focused on sustainability. Bon Appétit Management Company, where I lead brand strategy, falls into this category. Whereas Impossible Foods is single-minded in its mission to fight climate change, we exist to provide food services to corporations, private colleges, and specialty venues such as museums, but we want to do so in an ethical way and be known for our commitment to socially responsible practices. Deciding which practices and how to make them socially responsible has been key to building our brand equity. While Impossible Foods has a single filter, climate impact, that it uses to make decisions, we have many battles we're fighting, including animal welfare, farmworkers' rights, and environmental and community impacts. This makes picking our battles much more complex. We want to take on a wide range of meaningful initiatives, but we also need to create a succinct brand so our actions don't appear haphazard to outside observers, and we don't lose the battles because we're fighting on so many fronts simultaneously.

To successfully use a variety of issues to support your brand identity, layer multiple commitments that build on each other in the same area. Each initiative benefits from the credibility you've established with earlier successes (conversely, newer initiatives will also be more harshly scrutinized based on past missteps).

For a multipronged approach to be successful, your initiatives must be part of a greater narrative: your brand's story. Ben & Jerry's does this well. Under the banner of "Our Progressive Values," they lay out their multipronged approach to sustainability:

> Thoughtful Ingredients—Our ingredients support positive change and make our ice cream taste sensational!
>
> Shared Success—We aim to create prosperity for everyone that's connected to our business.
>
> Making a Difference—We build awareness and support for the activism causes we feel strongly about.[2]

This rubric has allowed the company to address issues spanning social and racial justice, global warming, fair labor, animal rights, and more without seeming like they were just throwing issues at the wall to see what sticks. Every commitment they make layers on top of the credibility they've built and fits into the single narrative they've carefully crafted: progressive values.

But Ben & Jerry's wide-swath approach also makes them accountable for a long list of societal ills. They're essentially saying that almost any problem, anywhere, is their responsibility. Rob Michalak learned about the complexity of that responsibility when serving as Ben & Jerry's global director of social mission and was forced to address one of the most complicated issues of our times, the Israel-Palestine conflict.

When you go into the business of making ice cream, you might never dream that peace in the Middle East will be on your daily to-do list. Take as sweeping and multipronged approach to sustainability as Ben & Jerry's has though, and you might find yourself, as Rob did in 2018, facing some incredibly sensitive issues. When we spoke, Rob explained:

> The Committee for a Just Peace in Israel and Palestine, and Vermonters for Peace in Palestine, came to us to say one of their members was in a supermarket in the occupied territories in the West Bank, and they got a pint of Ben & Jerry's. They said, "You need to pull your product out of there!" We said, "Ah OK, this is complicated."
>
> We had a licensee with rights to produce and distribute Ben & Jerry's within the Green Line, the demarcation that signified Israel in the 1940s. The problem is, though, once they sold their product to a distributor or supermarket chain, that company owns it, and they can put it wherever they want it.
>
> It was probably about 2 percent of the product that was being produced by our Israeli licensee that was getting into these markets in the West Bank, but the activists were saying, "You're profiting off the oppression of Palestinians." As it turned out, we at Ben & Jerry's really didn't make any money off that licensee arrangement at the time. There was a little bit of royalties, but it was a rounding error. . . . That was frustrating, but we heard what they were saying, and we understood the issues of justice as related to the Middle East.
>
> You come up against some of these things where you're trying to do the best you can, but given the complicated circumstances, trying to find the compromise might not be to the satisfaction of certain activist groups.

Eventually Ben & Jerry's informed the licensee that they would not renew the license agreement when it expired. Ben & Jerry's executives had taken a side in one of the most contentious debates in the world. Taking on that battle was in line with their brand. As Rob put it, "We said, 'Bring it on,' because our personality is to test and advocate for what we believe is just." (Read more from our conversation about how the company is structured to support their multipronged focus on page 80. It's the embodiment of the Ben & Jerry's brand story.)

Either of these approaches, single-minded or multipronged, will work, if you put in the work and you are authentic about what you're trying to achieve. Another way to frame this choice is between focusing on one issue or focusing on one story (more about telling that story in lesson five). For most of you, it will be the latter, and that story is your brand's sustainability identity—the foundation on which you can build.

Step Two: Identify Ideas for Initiatives

Building a credible brand based on sustainability will require a set of corporate initiatives that together add up to a clear point of view. The process of identifying the possible initiatives you could fit into your story takes time, patience, and fortitude.

The first step is to get out into the world and start listening. Instead of meeting suppliers in a boardroom, visit their sites. In my case, that means getting out to greenhouses, fields, or aquaculture facilities. For you, that could mean machine shops, server farms, or shipping centers. See how they operate. Look for common ground to work from. Most of all, speak directly with the people who make the things that make up your product. I speak directly with the people who raise the chickens we buy. You should talk to the workers in the factories or the journeymen on the jobsite. People on the front line. Look for policies and practices that could be controversial, bettered, or simply explained so the general public understands their importance.

Learn. Go to as many conferences as you can, whether they're for scientists, advocates, startups, government, or trade groups. Attend the standard sustainability gatherings such as the *Economist*'s annual

Sustainability Week and a Sustainable Brands event near you, and take a flier on something less mainstream like a Bioneers conference. You will meet people and find ideas for initiatives.

Look for journalists focused on sustainability who may know what emerging topics are soon to matter to your customers. In my world, I can name several such writers, like Barry Estabrook, Tom Philpott, Jane Black, and those writing for Civil Eats, the go-to site for sustainable-food news. Outside the food world, the same applies. Find your industry's activist voices or publications focused on cultural analysis and criticism such as *Dissent* magazine, a journal of the political left. You don't have to agree with these articles or journals; their ideas and writings will take a more extreme stance on most issues than you will be comfortable with, but they may seed an idea that you can form into something doable for your company, something unique that will set you apart as a leader.

Peruse the marketing materials of other companies in your industry or that supply your industry to see what battles they're picking. I look at big agriculture companies' marketing all the time. Reading between the lines tells me which issues they're playing defense against. For example, Tyson Foods' "Farmers" web page proudly states: "Contract poultry farming is not just the industry standard; it's also a relationship we believe works well for everyone."[3] Tyson seems to feel the need to defend contract poultry farming. That tips me off that there has been criticism of that system and there might be an initiative related to this area I want to focus on. Next, I could ask suppliers about their contracts, ground truth their response with an advocacy or watchdog group (on this issue, that's Farm Action, which aims to rebalance power in the US agriculture industry by calling out monopolistic practices). And I could use all of that information to craft an initiative that takes a stand for fairness and equity in our chicken supply chain, like demanding transparency in contracts.

Being the first company to take a stand could differentiate you from your competitors, give you a strong brand identity, and be great fodder for a thought leadership piece in a relevant news outlet or widely read trade magazine in your world. Sounds a lot like magic to me.

You never know where you'll make an important connection, spark a killer idea, or find inspiration for a new initiative. Research widely and then, once you have a preponderance of ideas, filter them through three lenses: your own passion, the advice of professional advocates, and your customers.

Lens One: Follow Your Passion—Even If It's Poop

The most obvious path to choosing which initiatives you launch from your list of ideas is to follow a personal passion. After all, believing market forces can be harnessed to make a better world is probably what drove you to want to create a brand based on sustainability. Initiatives fueled by passion will feed your soul and keep you engaged, which is good because they're also often laborious and involve exploring a lot of dead ends. You're going to have to survey the players, find the levers for change, and come up with your own solution. Initiatives based on your passions aren't usually your quick wins and they may not be marketable, but they have the potential to be important to you and to the world.

One of the things that kept me at Bon Appétit for thirty years is the latitude I had to explore issues that sparked my passion. While traveling and doing research to improve our supply chain, I often learned a new fact or had an experience that inspired me to create a new initiative. I was given the support to take a stand and create a program or policy. I knew that was a perk most employers wouldn't afford me. Never underestimate the retention value of letting someone follow their heart.

In some cases, how to address an issue you are passionate about is clear. After standing in a Salinas Valley romaine lettuce field covered in hundreds of pounds of discarded leaves that the harvesting crew had been taught were undesirable for customers, I was moved to create a food-waste-reduction initiative that included new culinary applications for otherwise undesirable produce. I knew our chefs would find creative ways to use what I dubbed "Imperfectly Delicious Produce." This was a clear-cut (or, rather, imperfectly cut, but clear) solution.

Other times, your passion won't be matched by clear paths forward. At a clandestine meeting at a Buddhist temple outside Bangkok with Burmese migrant workers who had escaped enslavement on fishing vessels, I saw a man's scarred ear from where he had been beaten with chains by his employer. I promised myself I would ensure that worker-safety hotlines are available throughout our supply chain. The passion was there, but I had no idea how to implement that safety precaution on ships on the high seas.

The idea of using my company's purchasing power to make a change for a cause that speaks to my heart is intoxicating. In reality, while these initiatives are important, they often move slowly and take a lot of patience. Often the most inspirational causes are complex. Much of my effort around slavery in the seafood supply chain falls into this category. As the daughter of two people who worked in the social services, I feel moved to fight for the less powerful. Helping to ensure people are being treated with respect and paid fairly for difficult, highly skilled work is more personally compelling to me than, say, ensuring the health of the wild salmon population.

However, the levers for change in labor issues are not as obvious as they are for reducing carbon emissions or ceasing the purchase of a certain species of fish. Without an obvious "buy this, not that" or "look for this certification," many of my actions to address seafood workers' rights have been aimed toward simply raising awareness of the issue rather than making difficult supply chain changes that I know will benefit workers, like the man with the mangled ear I met. The hope is that awareness will someday force an improvement in worker safety.

For now, the countless hours I've spent talking to seafood companies, advocates, and governmental agencies in multiple countries haven't resulted in a purchasing commitment. In the short term, though, all of that effort has built credibility for Bon Appétit. My engagement has shown the advocacy world that we are proactively involved in solving problems, not just reacting when directly asked for a specific change. As a brand, we get brownie points, and as an employee, my allegiance to Bon Appétit grows because the company supports my passion.

Fedele's passion for manure lagoons similarly fell into the category of an important issue without a clear path to a solution—and had the added challenge of being difficult to market. The putrid smell of pig poop propelled *his* desire to make change. Great!

Truly, it was great that the CEO of a company that buys millions of pounds of pork a year wanted to act. However, it would have to be behind the scenes; all the passion in the world won't make manure marketable at lunchtime.

The lack of a clear, direct, or quick payoff for some of these challenges doesn't mean you shouldn't take on personal passion projects. Quite the contrary. Just because we can't put pictures of manure on our marketing materials doesn't mean we should have continued buying from our shit-spraying purveyor. It's meaningful changes like our work on pork sourcing that builds credibility with those who deeply understand the issue. Your fervor will translate to authentic action, which will create goodwill, and you can put that on your balance sheet, if you know how. We may not sell more BLTs due to our good manure management, but we do sell more college and corporate business on the strength of our brand as the leader in sustainable food service.

In other cases, passion projects can be tweaked just a bit and yield big marketing results. One such example is the creation of Bon Appétit's Save Seafood Tour, which brought our desire to preserve the health of our oceans to customers across the country and highlighted our commitment in a totally new way. When the Monterey Bay Aquarium Seafood Watch team first told us about the sad state of global fish populations, they showed us a documentary called *Empty Oceans, Empty Nets*. The tales of illegal and unreported fishing and footage of thousands of pounds of dead or dying fish being thrown overboard, because the crude catch methods had ensnared unintended species as well as birds and marine mammals, made the decision to follow the Seafood Watch guidelines an easy choice. Fast-forward a few years later, a story about our new antibiotics policy for meat was getting wide attention, and I got a cold call from a man named Bob Silvestri with Environmental Media Fund who was looking for a sponsor for a film he was producing about the seafood industry. He figured since we were a company that cared about the food system, we'd be a good target for a funding request. Having no advertising budget, I turned him down and tried to end the call as quickly as I could—we preferred to spend our not-enormous food-service profits on local farms, cage-free eggs, higher-quality meat, and so on—but he kept talking: "The documentary we're making is the second in a series. The first was called *Empty Oceans, Empty Nets*." Needle drop! *"Empty Oceans, Empty Nets*?! We love *Empty Oceans, Empty Nets*! Maybe we do fund documentaries after all," I exclaimed. My passion was ignited.

What was the value to Bon Appétit, though? Having our logo alongside a list of other underwriters when the movie *Farming the Seas* played on PBS wasn't going to be worth the $25,000 Bob was asking for. Since our cafés aren't open to the public, a broadcasted message wouldn't be effective. We needed to ensure our specific clients and customers saw the film and noted our support.

In exchange for our sponsorship, Bob got the documentarians to make an eighteen-minute edit of the movie, including our logo, and we took it on the road: the Save Seafood Tour. At client locations across the country, we hosted evening events showing our exclusive cut of the film, followed by a panel discussion with me or another Bon Appétit rep, someone from Seafood Watch, and a local expert. Customers saw a Bon Appétiter sitting side by side with scientists and advocates working to save the oceans. We followed our passion—and then we found a way to market it.

If an initiative speaks to you, it will probably speak to others as well. And being able to channel personal passion builds credibility and authenticity for your brand. The ROI on passion is there. Pursue your passions because it's the right thing to do, and they will keep your company's spark alive in the long term.

A word of caution on bypassing passion: even though I'm say-ing passion projects are difficult, some true connection to a topic is important. If your interest in focusing on environmental and social benefits is purely mercenary—you think they're hot topics with con-sumers, but you don't feel personally passionate—stop here. Put down this book. Your brand will never be perceived as authentic. People can sense when they're being played.

Lens Two: Ask the Advocates

For initiatives with clearer, more direct paths than those of passion projects, look to your professional advocate partners—or find some. For us it could be the Humane Society of the United States or Seafood Watch, or others. The success of most advocacy campaigns rests heav-ily on changing the practices of large companies, so they'll most likely be excited to work with you. The benefits of signing on to an advo-cate's ask include access to experts who understand the issues and can educate you (of course they're advocates, so they'll present the infor-mation that furthers their cause), and who can outline impactful next steps that will lead to meaningful change, and—bonus—they'll be sure to tout your actions.

Working with professional advocates often lays out a set of actions and lets you grab a free ride on the PR engine of a potentially sophisti-cated third party. Case in point: at Bon Appétit, our first lesson about the world of reducing antibiotics use in farm animals came at the knee of the Environmental Defense Fund (EDF). They provided a project manager who put together a coalition of several noncompeting restau-rant companies that were all interested in reducing the public health threat caused by antibiotic resistance, and they brought potential sup-pliers to the table as well. The EDF science team taught me and my colleagues why antibiotics are given to healthy animals, how bacteria develop resistance, and how this reduces the efficacy of medically important drugs for humans.

I remember saying to a group of our chefs, "When you went into cooking, I bet you didn't think you'd be back in Bio 101 and using scary words like methicillin-resistant *Staphylococcus aureus*." I wouldn't have been able to use those words correctly myself, much less write an effective policy, without the guidance of EDF. Oh, and the EDF media team got coverage for our collective work in major national newspapers, too.

Working with EDF showed me the advantages of taking an advocacy group's lead in picking an issue and fully leaning on the resources and knowledge they can bring to the table. A handful of meetings with an advocacy group project manager, and we essentially got a biology teacher and policy consultants with a free PR team to boot. Who's your EDF? Is it a plastics watchdog that knows the packaging business? Labor experts who advocate against unfair practices? Maybe it's a renewable energy organization that has done the calculations on solar and wind power conversion from coal.

I've followed this model again and again with great success and suggest you do the same. However, there are two common mistakes companies make when advocacy groups come calling:

Mistake one: They treat advocacy groups as adversaries.

Mistake two: They rush to placate them.

The knee-jerk reaction of most businesses is to clam up when advocates approach. Loud PETA protests in front of KFC restaurants, the Coalition of Immokalee Workers staging a hunger strike outside Taco Bell headquarters, and Greenpeace releasing its *Carting Away the Oceans* report without a single retailer receiving a passing score were all designed to scare companies into making change. And they worked. Companies fear the wrath of advocacy groups. All these activist stunts and the ensuing bad publicity could've been avoided, however, if the companies treated the advocates as partners rather than adversaries.

Relationships with advocates should be a two-way street. Don't keep them at arm's length. Instead, invite them to get to know you, your business, and your challenges. These are people who have dedicated their professional lives to a specific topic. They think about this one issue all day, every day. (Well, let's hope they sleep, too, but in my experience, people who choose to be professional advocates spend most of their waking hours fighting for their cause.)

Don't be afraid of even those organizations with cantankerous reputations. I successfully partnered with Greenpeace and got them to give a supporting quote in our press release about banning plastic straws. We won awards from PETA for the "Most Vegetarian Conscious Ball Park" and "Most Vegetarian and Earth-Friendly Corporate Café." Those endorsements carry a huge amount of credibility specifically because Greenpeace and PETA are known for campaigning against corporations. Instead of treating advocacy groups like the enemy, think of them as free consultants and PR machines.

Yes, the Center for Science in the Public Interest (CSPI) has sued several companies—they even have a page on their website dedicated to their work "In the Courts"—so it's tempting to run away when you might cross paths with them. On the flip side, imagine the power of a positive mention from someone at CSPI. They're incredibly trusted by their followers. The CSPI *Nutrition Action* newsletter goes out to 900,000 paid subscribers. Almost a million people trust them enough to spend money on their science-based content. When CSPI cites your company's work as a positive example, that's a powerful endorsement. So don't run from CSPI and the like; embrace them.

Part of this is just the economics of wanting to do sustainability right. Seafood Watch employs thirty-five or so scientists in ten countries. I employ zero. Essentially, I outsource my research needs in seafood to them, at no cost to me. For example, when another partner, Johns Hopkins Center for a Livable Future, recommended we take a stand on antibiotics use in aquaculture, my next call was to Seafood Watch. Within days I was hooked up with an expert, someone who has spent hundreds of hours asking questions and reading and writing reports on chemical use in fish farming. I would never be able to duplicate that knowledge in-house.

I was able to make that call to Seafood Watch because I have spent years cultivating this relationship and not treating them like an adversary. As I said, it's a two-way street. When Seafood Watch is looking for corporate signatories on a letter to a regional fisheries-management organization, I'm always the first to say yes. When they need a speaker at a blue swimming crab conference, I'm ready with a PowerPoint that stresses, among other points, how closely our corporate purchasing standards follow Seafood Watch guidelines. And when it asks for someone to be on camera, even after a very long day touring shrimp farms in the steaming hot Thai countryside, I wipe off the sweat, don't worry about my hair or (lack of) makeup, and give the best sound bite I can while standing on a noisy street corner in Bangkok. Because I want the Seafood Watch team to think of us every time it needs an example of a good corporate citizen.

I have a similar relationship with a half dozen other organizations. Please don't mistake what I'm saying for simple quid pro quo. These are real, tried-and-true relationships built over years of working together toward common goals with transparency on both sides. When I want to tackle a new subject, I immediately look for an advocacy group with deep expertise in the area. They can help me craft policy, act as my first (and most educated) focus group to see how the commitment will play externally, and they'll eventually be a great way to publicize the announcement—either through their own PR channels or by lending a credible quote to a press release.

They're also my partners in problem-solving. When I don't know the path to meeting a promise, like Compassion in World Farming's Better Chicken Commitment, I lay out the challenges I'm facing to the advocates themselves as early as possible. I'm juggling initiatives for chicken, seafood, farmworkers, carbon reduction, and more, but Compassion has staff dedicated to figuring out how to make slow-growing chickens feasible for the mass market. That assistance is golden.

Not all these relationships come easy. In January 2009 we received a certified letter with a return-receipt request that highlighted the Coalition of Immokalee Workers (CIW) and information about their Fair Food Program. It didn't have a specific ask. The letter was signed by an entire page of organizations, including a lot of religious groups and farmworker advocates, but no one person. Clearly someone wanted to prove we'd received the information but was very unclear what they wanted us to do with it.

I started with the top of the list and called each group until I connected with Greg Asbed, one of the founders of the CIW. He told me that 90 percent of tomatoes that are sold east of the Mississippi in the winter months come out of the area of Florida around Immokalee, which has been called "Ground Zero for modern-day slavery" by a federal prosecutor. There had been seven prosecuted cases of slavery in Immokalee in the years right up to that letter. He demanded we join the Fair Food Program and require all tomato growers who sold to us to sign a code of conduct that included Bon Appétit paying an additional penny per pound that would get passed directly to the farmworkers.

Greg opened our conversation with a demand, I later learned, because the requests he and the CIW had made to other corporations hadn't been met with much courtesy, let alone friendly agreement. Taco Bell, McDonald's, and others had signed on to the Fair Food Agreement only after CIW had staged protests, multiday marches, and even hunger strikes. No company had simply said yes . . . until we did.

I did my research, of course. I went there. Entering Immokalee for our first meeting with CIW was like leaving the United States that I knew. Located less than an hour from upscale Naples, vultures (yes, vultures, the bird of prey, apropos in a community also preyed upon by unscrupulous people) walked the dusty streets as tumbleweeds rolled by. Workers lived packed tight in ramshackle mobile homes, for which they paid steep rents, in exchange for proximity to a parking lot at which they gathered each day at 4 a.m. in hopes of securing a shift in the fields. We walked by the empty lot, just blocks from the CIW office, where a U-Haul truck had held men captive and led to the most recent slavery prosecution. Those workers had been brought into the United States by "coyotes," people who smuggle immigrants across the US-Mexico border, charging them exorbitant amounts of money so they arrive deep in debt. If they flee, associates of the coyotes back in Mexico threaten the families left behind.

Of course, I was moved. Of course, we were going to sign on to the Fair Food Program. Still, I could feel CIW members' suspicion of our corporate motives. We spent two days together, talking, learning about the issues and each other, and coming to an agreement without much to argue about. Even though Bon Appétit agreed to do everything they asked, I left knowing we still had to prove ourselves to these people fighting every day for their basic rights.

Over the ensuing years, I've continued to try to demonstrate our sincerity to the members of CIW. When there was an action in my hometown, I had the whole group over to my house for dinner. I marched for three days in Florida while carrying signs and chanting demands for justice. I sent cakes to their office to mark their anniversary, featured their campaigns in our cafés, and told film director Sanjay Rawal their story, sparking the idea for Sanjay's moving documentary *Food Chains*, which debuted at the Tribeca Film Festival.

My relationship with CIW is one I value highly because of my immense respect for what they've achieved. It's one that I consciously foster and don't take for granted. It reminds me that we make these commitments because of the advocates' cause, not to get a thank-you or a plaque from the NGO saying so.

Working with advocacy groups can be a symbiotic relationship for a sustainability-focused company. It takes work, communication, and transparency, but the returns—in terms of both knowledge and reputation—are worth it. (Read about how much Ernie Farley of Good Farms has gained by partnering with the United Farm Workers, which he once considered an adversary, in the interview on page 54.)

Avoid mistake number one, but also keep in mind that advocacy groups are skilled at the hard sell. Don't make mistake number two and rush to sign on the dotted line just to placate them. First weigh what you think is possible to achieve against the competitive landscape.

If an advocacy group is wooing you, you can be sure they're also having the same conversation with your competitors. Signing a commitment to a new sourcing practice that everyone else in your industry is also signing may add up to industrywide change, but it's not going to create differentiation for you. Don't fall into the trap of trying to stand out simply by being the first to sign. Professional advocates know sustainability has become a race of sorts, and they'll smartly play that to their advantage by dangling the carrot of being first while waving the stick of being left behind the pack.

Rushing to be first can lead to rash decisions. I witnessed one such stampede toward sustainability fueled by a Nicholas Kristof–penned exposé in the *New York Times* featuring a Perdue Farms contract chicken producer. (I asked Jim Perdue, chairman of Perdue Farms, about this article in our interview on page 49.) On the heels of the high-profile piece, Compassion in World Farming put together their Better Chicken Commitment. They asked food-service companies to adopt a purchasing policy for chicken that addresses issues related to bird health by 2024. Basically, the policy requires fewer birds, in barns with more bells and whistles, and most importantly, a slower-growing breed of chicken.

Unfortunately, when Compassion in World Farming made the ask in 2016, "slower growing" didn't have a clear definition—the breeds had not yet been fully identified, much less put into production—so costs were impossible to determine. But 2024 seemed like a long way away, and the photos of the overly buxom chickens, their breasts too big and their legs too underdeveloped to walk properly, were heartbreaking. And the Compassion folks were persuasive, telling me and my counterparts at each company that we could make history by signing first.

The first to jump was Compass Group, my company's parent company. Lots of congratulations went around, as everyone was excited by the bold step taken by the world's largest food-service company. Compass immediately spurred others to step up to the plate. Major competitor Aramark released its commitment literally hours later. Compassion had a lot of companies queued up and watching. In short order, the whole food-service industry and others from around the food world jumped on board: more than two hundred companies including Sodexo, IKEA, Burger King, General Mills, and Nestlé.

Chicken-leg health was on the agenda!

But again, no one knew how much it was going to cost to make this promise a reality, nor how much more land and feed it would take to allow chickens to live longer, creating additional environmental and financial costs.

The University of Guelph did a study of sixteen genetic strains of chicken, fitting them with wearable devices, like mini chicken Fitbits, and compared mobility and activity. The researchers set up an obstacle test to compare leg strength among different poultry strains and monitored the birds' use of enrichment items while examining for foot lesions. They also looked at meat quality, because—oh, yeah—these are bred to be eaten. Based on that work, in 2020, they released a list of breeds—including Hubbard Black, JA757, 787, 957, or 987; Rambler Ranger, Ranger Classic, or Ranger Gold—that met the commitment. Huzzah!

Small problem: no one is yet raising those breeds on an industrial scale or at a price that any of the signatory companies are willing to pay. And I don't mean pay more when the promise comes due in 2024 and they can switch over their supply chains to slow-grow chickens then. I mean they would've had to start paying in 2021 to convert the breed to meet the 2024 deadline. Due to an explanation of genetics and "grandparent stock" that I confess I've never truly understood, it takes three years to introduce new genetics into a system—even though the chickens live less than forty-five days. In other words, if you wanted compliant chicken in 2024, you would have started paying by 2021.

Given the time it took to determine the proper parameters, Compassion extended the deadline for the breed change to 2026 to give producers and buyers time to make deals and grow out a new chicken supply. Still, as of early 2023, no company purchasing a large amount of chicken has stepped forward to make their commitment a reality.

By my math, every single one of those two hundred companies is going to be unable to fully reach their promise, including my own. If history is an indicator, the animal welfare groups are going to go from singing our praises to pointing out our "lies." Instead of a point of pride to brag about on corporate websites, the Better Chicken Commitment will be a black eye that companies will cover up and hope their customers don't ask about. We're headed for embarrassment, to say the least. And the chickens will still be growing faster than their legs can properly hold them up.

Playing chicken with advocacy groups and your competitors is a dangerous game. The advantage you get by picking a hot issue can quickly disappear if advocacy groups are also simultaneously working with your competitors, or if you're not able to live up to a commitment you make. You may enjoy a brief halo for making a promise, but it's quickly going to tarnish if you don't—or can't—take action toward meaningful change. That doesn't mean you've got to have a crystal ball and have everything figured out before committing to take on an issue. In my experience, to be seen as a true leader, you've got to take some risks and sometimes leap before you look.

The takeaway here? Build a stable of trusted advocate advisers, with whom you have real relationships that are transparent and two-way, and be willing to take some big risks. Do the research and go out on a limb for issues you believe in—not because you have an advocate pressuring you.

Lens Three: Listen to Your Customers

I rarely get well-formed ideas from customers. They don't fully understand our business or spend enough time thinking about it to present a formal, doable request like a professional advocate does. So I don't expect customers to help me write our purchasing policies or push for change in ways that are practical. But I do listen deeply to their feedback, especially from the most sustainably conscious customers. These well-informed consumers are great for directional guidance.

A brand built around sustainability must be thinking ahead, out in front of almost everyone else, including most consumers. Listening to the most die-hard activists among your customers is a useful way to see what minefields lie ahead and plot a course through. Movements start with a few extreme believers—and if you let them, they can be your North Star. Or at least one of the many stars you chart when picking issues to take on.

By listening to the types of questions customers are asking, you get a peek into what types of policies and campaigns will resonate with them. For example, the most frequent question I get after speaking to customers or the general public can usually be summarized as "Where can I shop and know that everything I buy there is ethical/sustainable/'good'?"

Translation: people don't want to have to spend extra time reading labels at the grocery store or asking questions of their waiter. They'd rather not have to research or make decisions themselves. They want to believe someone at the company is doing all that for them. They really, really want to be able to trust the brand. I do not hear "What questions can I ask at the seafood counter to know if the fish is sustainable?" but rather "If I go to Whole Foods, will all the fish be sustainable?"

Even misguided questions from customers are signals for issues they care about. While doing a speaking gig for Earth Day at a biotech company my company served, I was met with a spate of questions about our chicken: "How can I get gluten-free chicken?" "Is your chicken given hormones?" and "Is the chicken you serve cage-free?" Easy! Gluten is a protein found in certain cereal grains, so no, it is not in our chicken. The FDA doesn't allow added hormones in chicken production, and all chickens raised for meat are raised cage-free; cages are used for egg-laying hens.

What those questions told me, though, was that even these well-educated guests with backgrounds in science didn't really understand the sustainability issues they cared about, but I knew from what they asked that they were concerned about allergens, additives, and animal welfare. Those are all issues I should consider taking on, and my marketing materials surrounding those initiatives are going to have to be straightforward and easy to understand.

Learning that guests want a general feeling of assurance spurred our "You're Already Doing Something Great" campaign at Bon Appétit. We commissioned an infographic illustrating all the positive impacts on the environment and community that guests were supporting just by eating in our cafés. They didn't have to do anything but have lunch to benefit farmers, farmworkers, the soil, the ocean, and animal welfare. No questions from them required.

Chipotle's "Food with Integrity" platform also does a terrific job of this. Customers need not Google things on their phone while waiting online to make the sustainable choice when ordering their burrito. Chipotle promises them that they've done the proper sourcing already, from the pork that supports family farmers to the beans that are transitioning land to organic production. This doesn't mean they're greenwashing by putting up inaccurate representations of their company. They're doing the work for their customers, letting them know they can be trusted, and backing up their claims with detailed sustainability reporting on their website, if anyone wants proof.

University students are my go-to source for understanding where the mind of the public is headed. College is often a time when people push boundaries and challenge authority, and corporations are seen today as more influential authority figures than elected officials. Students are flexing their independence and power, often with little concern for practicality. They want to break down norms and change the world. I'm not complaining. It's an inspiring population to serve. Plus, these college students will literally be my customers in some of the corporate accounts we cater to, at companies like Google and LinkedIn, when they graduate.

To connect with students, I accept as many speaking gigs on campuses as I can. I see who shows up to my talks and read the reactions in the room as I delve into different issues that either we've already made commitments about or I'm considering for action. I try to stir up conversation or even debate by bringing up the issues that I think students may be critical of, such as bottled water, to see if anyone suggests a plastic-bottle ban or mentions that Dasani is owned by Coca-Cola and cites the "Killer Coke Campaign" formed after the soft drink bottler was accused of human rights atrocities in Colombia. It's a subtle way to check interest on initiatives I'm considering.

To keep the conversation with students flowing, I created a fellowship for recent graduates who were student activists at any of the colleges we serve. The Bon Appétit Fellows travel the country doing peer-to-peer education on sustainability. Every time a Fellow does a college visit, I have them jot down the questions the students ask. Knowing if eighteen-year-olds are focused more on climate change, animal welfare, or farmworkers gives me a sense of which policies my target audience would see as meaningful. It's the best focus group in the world because the students aren't influenced by knowing they're being studied.

To gather feedback from the full breadth of our customers, we also have comment forms on all our café websites, and someone on my team shares with me a sense of the areas of guests' concerns. I'm personally blind-copied on any inquiry to info@bamco.com so I see what's risen to such a level of concern that customers have sought out our corporate email address. From this I've learned of brewing interest in GMOs, canola oil, and local purchasing. I even pay attention to the complaint emails we receive that are meant for *Bon Appétit* magazine but are mistakenly sent to us by confused readers. (The biggest issue there, apparently, is missteps in finding the right balance between cultural appreciation, appropriation, and what's negatively perceived as "wokeness" in recipes.) Seeing what sets off the magazine readers is another useful data point for me in deciding which issues we should prepare our culinary teams for.

Listen to the people who reach out to you—all of them. That includes those who are underinformed, barely able to vote, and not your customers at all. Each one provides valuable insight into what people care about and how you can meet them exactly where they are.

Advocacy groups have also figured out that college students are an influential force. For example, Fair Trade Campaigns, an organization founded to mobilize consumers to demand an increase in the avail-ability of Fair Trade products, has a specific division dedicated to uni-versity action, of which I've been a longtime adviser.

Even if an advocacy group doesn't have a formal college cam-paign, passionate students may have a personal tie to a particular organization, another place to look when picking your battles. It's a one-two punch of pressure from a customer request plus a profes-sional campaigner. One of the battles we picked, which turned into a big win, was the direct result of this combination of a customer and an advocate.

It started with one question asked by one student. You can make huge gains in your sustainability program just by listening for single questions like this one. In 2005, David Benzaquen at American Univer-sity asked our then–general manager, Yvonne Matteson, if the campus could have cage-free eggs in its dining halls.

Yvonne had never heard of cage-free eggs, so she called me and said, "Can we get cage-free eggs?" I had never heard of them either.

David put me in contact with the Humane Society, where I met Josh Balk, who has turned out to be one of my greatest allies in keeping Bon Appétit at the leading edge of animal welfare issues. We have since worked together for twenty years on countless initiatives and provided each other strategic advice (see page 165 for an interview with Josh). But back then, I just needed to know about cage-free eggs. He sent me a VHS tape by mail. I asked Marc Zammit, who oversaw chef train-ing and was my partner in new sourcing initiatives, if he wanted to watch some footage of hens with me. "Honestly, I don't know if I even care about chickens," I added. "I mean chickens aren't puppies. We're raising them to eat anyway."

We watched seven minutes of sickly looking chickens in barren battery cages, their heads stuck through the wires, immobilized and unable to even drink. They were packed in layer upon layer of cages stacked to the ceiling, so their feces were falling on the birds below them. We were aghast. I turned to Marc and said, "Chickens *are* like puppies. I care about chickens."

The most obvious lesson here is that one person making a request can spur change, and that's true and important. Even more so, it was the combination of David and the machine that is the Humane Society behind him that forced us to listen.

Yes, I was emotionally moved, and that created the will in me to convince others that cage-free eggs were worth paying more for, but I also could tell that a campaign was burgeoning. David wasn't just an individual student who decided to approach his campus food-service provider. He was the first of a group of young activists working with the Humane Society. He was a signal in the noise, an indication that something was brewing. This was the battle that launched Bon Appétit's brand into a public sphere that we, as a primarily business-to-business company, hadn't played in before. By listening to a single customer and not shying away from partnering with an activist organization, I created an initiative that made for an authentic differentiation in the market and earned us attention from the media, clients, and guests for years to come.

Pay attention to patterns. A college student talking about an issue is one thing, but a college student and an advocacy group ready with a video are two connected points of data. A pattern was emerging indicating a budding issue, a great opportunity to be the first to launch an initiative many more people would come to care about later. That's a good battle to pick.

Step Three: Manage Your Portfolio of Ideas

When you allow yourself to follow your own passions, cultivate relationships with advocacy groups, and seek signals from your most extreme-thinking customers, you're going to be inspired to create more initiatives than you can handle. You will have multiple battles to choose from. An idea will strike when you're not ready to take on a new project, or you'll do research on a topic and hit a roadblock—maybe a lack of available information, steep costs, or a supply constraint.

Picking battles will not be a linear process. You'll need a system for organizing ideas that captures all the possible initiatives that arise while not letting pie-in-the-sky dreams distract you from solutions you need to act on today. There is a lot to balance. Big, complex issues like slavery in the seafood supply chain need to be kept front of mind, because commitments in such areas can take years to develop and require coming back to again and again. Once you make a commitment, you need to tend to it lest you fall out of step with your own promises as suppliers change, economics adjust, and so forth. What feels crazy today, like getting rid of plastic straws, may seem doable tomorrow. And an issue that seems threatening, such as GMO salmon, might fizzle in the marketplace. Organize and keep track of your potential battles as a portfolio of options and projects so you don't risk falling back on your commitments or miss an opportunity to make meaningful change.

At Bon Appétit, we developed a "Circle of Responsibility (COR) matrix" to track commitments and ideas. The COR matrix is a spreadsheet that we pull out at quarterly meetings and every time we find ourselves naturally discussing our brand positioning as related to sustainability, which is a near-weekly topic in leadership meetings. It helps us prioritize and track issue ideas using the stoplight system:

Green: commitments we've publicly made

Yellow: commitments in progress

Red: issues we want to take on but can't yet

You'll want all categories to be growing in number. The desire for more green commitments is obvious. You want to be making real promises and telling the world about them. Large yellow and red lists are critical to leadership, too, though.

Yellow is where the active work is being done. Creating and implementing a new policy isn't usually a quick process. To keep a steady drumbeat of green commitments, you need a very active yellow section. For example, if you'd like to make a new commitment publicly every six months, you'll probably need to be working on at least twice as many possible policies: something is always bound to take longer than anticipated or forces will shift in unexpected ways, reordering your agenda items.

It might seem counterintuitive to think you want a long red list. After all, red is where you're stuck. It's a list of initiatives that you don't know how to move forward on. But red is where the real leadership is. If you don't know how to take action, neither does your competition. These are the hard nuts to crack, the problems without obvious answers, the costs you can't figure out how to cover. Here is where brands are built.

Pull out your matrix regularly (at least quarterly but probably more than that), discuss, debate, throw out crazy ideas, and dream. Ask yourself for each item:

Green	Yellow	Red
Are we on track to meet all these commitments?	What's stopping us from moving each yellow item to green?	Are there any outside experts we could tap to get us started?
Are these commitments still leading the industry, or have our competitors caught up?	What else do we need to know before we can make a public commitment?	Have any companies outside of our set of direct competitors taken a stand on these issues? What can we learn from their approaches?
Are these commitments in line with current science and best thinking?	Is there any external time pressure such as a looming law, advocacy campaign, or fear that a competitor will move first?	Is there a baby step we could take?
		Would a commitment in this area be marketable?

Knowing which specific issue is going to resonate with your customers is more an art than a science. If an issue is important to you, it'll probably speak to others. If an advocacy group is campaigning for corporate change, they're probably also drumming up interest with their members or supporters. And if even one guest asks about an issue, there are probably many more of your customers who would appreciate action. That's a lot of "probably." The only thing I know for sure is that leadership requires *action*. You've got to pick an issue, make a commitment, see how the world receives it, adjust, pick another issue, and build, build, build your brand.

Picking your battles may lead you to unexpected places. It's led me to that shower stall in rural Pennsylvania, changing underwear to get ready for my date with thousands of pregnant pigs. It's put me in tense conversations with customers. It's pulled me from manure lagoons to gestation crates. The key I've found to not getting lost in my search for the right battle is to be an active listener. Listen to the people in the community, the ones suffering from poop being sprayed outside their window. Listen to the activists and the organizations they trust. Listen to your customers. Listen to the suppliers. Listen to your passions. Listen and you'll find the magic.

ACTION ITEMS

How to Pick Your Battles

Building a brand known for authentically promoting sustainability requires both making meaningful change and getting market recognition for your efforts. This starts with strategically picking the area or areas in which your company will show leadership.

You'll need to find an issue or set of issues that all your stakeholders, employees, customers, and the press can easily grasp. No matter your industry, these steps will guide you in picking *your* battle:

Step one: Find your focus. Determine if your brand will focus on a single issue and dive deep or take a multipronged approach and be known for general sustainability.

Step two: Identify ideas for initiatives. Go out into the world and start listening for inspiration. You may have a personal passion fueling your work and you'll need to see if it resonates with your target market or, if you're searching for ideas, you'll want to listen to professional advocates and everyday customers to determine which actions to take. Make sure the set of initiatives you choose collectively adds up to a cohesive, noteworthy story.

Step three: Manage your portfolio of ideas so you can take on the right battles at the right time. If you're doing a great job listening to a variety of sources, you're going to come up with more ideas than you can effectively tackle at once. Organize and track each initiative as it moves from harebrained scheme to active planning to public promise and, finally, to achievement of the goal. This discipline will keep you from falling back on your commitments or missing your chance to make meaningful change and get market credit.

Interview

Picking Battles by Following Your Passion

GARY HIRSHBERG

Cofounder, Stonyfield Organic

Gary Hirshberg is a pioneer of purpose-driven business, having used activism to create the country's leading organic yogurt brand. His impact is felt far and wide as he's the author of *Stirring It Up: How to Make Money and Save the World*, has received twelve honorary doctorates and numerous awards for corporate and environmental leadership, including a Lifetime Achievement Award by the US Environmental Protection Agency, and runs the Hirshberg Entrepreneurship Institute, a high impact three-day boot camp.

Gary and I talked about how he took on a slate of environmental issues as well as some surprising non-food-related causes, which were born out of his passion, and the challenges of doing that. (This interview, along with all the others in this book, has been edited for length and clarity.)

Which came first, the sustainability issue or the yogurt?

Before we'd ever thought of selling yogurt, Samuel Kaymen, eventual cofounder of Stonyfield and creator of the yogurt recipe, and I were both running nonprofits in the advocacy world. Samuel's was an organic farming school and mine was a sort of twenty-first-century, sustainable systems, education, and research place, working on climate change and reducing waste. We were proving the ecological benefits of our approaches—improving biodiversity, sequestering carbon, reducing water use, improving animal health—but the one thing we were not proving was the economics of it. Can people actually make a living or afford to grow and eat this way? And so, we were kind of enchanted with the idea of doing a business to find that out.

How do you pick which issues to take on at Stonyfield?

We were opposed to the whole idea of ignoring the externalities of Western civilization, so that's a pretty big funnel of issues to choose from. The honest answer is, we moved on what moved us. For example, I learned that nineteen kids were dying every day in America from gun violence and decided to support a group called Stop Handgun Violence. And we put that on the lids of our yogurt cups.

We viewed these causes that we cared about as a two-way street: it was a way of identifying our customers, the people who we thought would be more supportive of organic products, bigger thinkers, the "question authority" generation. Taking on these issues gave us an excuse to speak to these people directly and build a relationship with our customers.

We had almost no marketing budget, so we used whatever we had to promote the issues we cared about. We had this "Moosletter, All the Moos that's Fit to Print" that we sent out by mail, because there was no email yet. And then we also used our lids.

It was a symbiotic relationship. We weren't taking on causes that we didn't believe in ourselves. It was very personal. But we also saw the question-authority generation becoming consumers and having the power to use their dollars to redirect commerce. So this was our way of choosing issues and then our means of promoting them, because we were growing a business, too.

Did this approach help you compete with larger companies?

We knew we couldn't compete with the marketing budgets of other manufacturers. My *gross* margins were worse than the *net* margins of the competition. We figured that we could use our skills as educational activists to promote the business.

And the flip side: Did you worry about alienating potential customers?

Well, we probably should have, but no, we didn't. Our attitude was the world was getting messed up. We were warming the planet, polluting the planet, agriculture was failing, and all the externalities were coming home. We were using up water, the rich were getting richer, the poor were getting poorer, and kids were dying from gun violence. We just figured if people didn't like our issues, then they probably wouldn't buy our yogurt. But we figured nobody would fault us for trying to make the world a better place. We were wrong about that. Some did fault us. The gun thing was a big problem. We got clobbered with mail from NRA [National Rifle Association] members.

One of my issues was campaign finance reform. I had this lid that said, "In politics, the cream doesn't always rise to the top," and when you flipped it over, it was advocating for campaign finance reform. That lid debuted the week that the food-service buyer on Capitol Hill had brought our yogurt into its café. I didn't do that intentionally.

I got four cases of our yogurt returned with a note that said, "These lids were too political for Capitol Hill," which I always thought was hilarious.

Still you managed to grow a brand while acting on your sustainability ambitions.

I'd love to tell you I knew what I was doing. I didn't. I learned that in consumer products, reach [how many customers you have] and frequency [how often they buy your product] are the ways you improve your gross margins. The traditional mentality is do as much advertising as possible to get as much reach and as much frequency as you can. You just hit people with impressions—Super Bowl ads, whatever—which we obviously couldn't do with our budget. But that conventional way of thinking is not actually correct, because the most powerful influence on people's purchase habits is word of mouth, not advertisement. It's hearing from someone. And word of mouth is a direct result of somebody having an emotional connection with your brand. Nobody talks about a brand if they weren't touched by it—touched in the heart, not in the head.

By attaching yourself to issues, there is the risk of alienating people who don't agree with you, but it also has the benefit of driving not just interest but excitement, enthusiasm, loyalty, and word of mouth with the audience who does care about your issues. I would counsel people not to shy away from picking an issue. It's a secret weapon, particularly when you have produced better products, and therefore, your price is not going to be as competitive.

How do you take on issues like climate change, when your product is made from methane-producing cows, or talk about waste, when you have a plastic package? Can you take on an issue if you're part of the problem?

Everyone has a footprint—water, packaging, and energy. It's all about continuous improvement and lowering the footprint. We have cows, and people should be eating fewer animal products, but they should be eating better when they do eat animal products. And they should be eating from farms that do more ecosystem services like ours. Our farmers have eighty cows on average, so their footprints are small. Their cows are also required to have access to pasture, so their methane output is much lower. And by raising them organically, manure is going to be a big part of how we restore our depleted farmland.

As for plastic cups, there are many, many things I'm really proud of, but if there's one gigantic thing I'm not, it's that we never solved the packaging problem. I always say that the holy grail will be when you finish eating the yogurt, you eat the cup.

That would be novel, and sustainable.

I did produce an edible package at one point. We made a yogurt in these things called wikis, which were little like pearls, like a grape. It was a skin that was a bunch of enzymes that when working together became impervious to water, so they could hold yogurt. You could pop them in your mouth and eat them.

It was a hard thing to get into the supermarket because consumers couldn't understand eating something without plastic around it. They don't think twice about picking up a pear or an apple, but they couldn't understand picking up a little yogurt ball. We tried it for a few years. It was a good effort.

Our main achievement has not been in the materials we use but in the amount of material and its weight. It's the lightest weight we could manage while remaining durable and recyclable, even though recycling is not really the solution.

We were up front about what we weren't doing right. And we were also up front about what we were working on. We never set out to just talk about stuff. We set out to model the behavior. I can't think of an issue that we ever talked about, that we weren't doing ourselves. On gun safety, we gave out trigger locks to our employees. On nuclear power, we bought wind energy for our factory. We walk the talk.

It isn't just about picking an issue. It's about doing it credibly and transparently. Not saying you're perfect. Not saying you're better, and they're bad. It's about saying this is what you're working on, and people are welcome to come kick the tires because you know that where you are now is good and you have a lot further to go.

Picking Battles by Listening to Customers, Critics, and Advocates

JIM PERDUE
Chairman, Perdue Farms

Frank Perdue is credited with creating the first brand-name chicken. Serving as the commercial face in television, print, and radio ads for the eponymous company his father started, he often ended by saying, "It takes a tough man to make a tender chicken," and asking customers to contact him personally with complaints. His son, Jim, has been chairman since 1991 and is equally as tough in his obsession with customer satisfaction. As he said in his commercial debut: "I have to be. My name and money-back guarantee are on every bird I sell."

I first met Jim after I'd made some pointed remarks about "Big Chicken," at a meeting held by Compassion in World Farming. Jim did not attack me or dismiss me for this, though. Instead, he invited me to speak at a Perdue board of directors meeting so his board could hear how their industry is perceived and what I thought should be done about it.

The radical commitment to tough feedback is alive and well, including in the fourth generation of Perdues who are now taking the helm.

How do you decide which issues of sustainability to take on as a company?

One thing my dad taught me and the whole company was to look outward, not inward. Especially look to the consumer. He always said if you listen to the consumer, you'll produce the kind of quality products they want; you'll succeed. And that's it. Everybody says that, but it's very, very true and it's very difficult.

One of my jobs is always to make sure we're not looking inward at what's easiest for us to do versus what the consumer wants, because it's more complicated and more difficult once you ask the consumer what they want. An example of that is NAE [raising chickens with No Antibiotics Ever]. We did that because the consumer kept asking us to.

We get about nine thousand contacts a month from customers. Most of them are complaints, which we love, because that's how we find out when we've got problems in our products. We also get a lot of comments, because we have a loyal base that stays in touch with us, and they bring up issues. What are you doing about this? What's in your product? What kind of oil do you fry in? This new generation is much less trusting than the baby boomers. Baby boomers trusted companies and businesses to do the right thing, which wasn't necessarily right. Millennials and Gen Z are much more critical and ask a ton of questions.

So that's where we get a lot of the impetus for things that we want to do—based on what customers say. We have a meeting once a month where we go through what they are telling us, what we are learning from these consumers. All the senior management is involved in those meetings, to keep us focused on where we should be, which is on the consumer.

Are consumers always willing to pay more for the things they're asking about?

We try to make the change a benefit in many ways. An example is the environmental impact of the trays the chicken comes on. Chicken comes on a Styrofoam tray, and we were scrambling to figure out what we're going to put the chicken in. Turns out, some of the recyclable plastic–type materials make for a better-looking package. We think we can actually sell more product by being in a better-looking tray than a Styrofoam one. That's on top of the environmental benefit.

How much of what you do is based on objective research and how much is based on a gut feeling?

With our Animal Care Initiative, we were in a meeting with Leah Garces, who was then with Compassion in World Farming. She told us, "These are things we'd like to see you do, but we don't know if it's economically feasible." That's our job to find out if it's economically feasible. So now we're in the pasture-growing business.

My son lives in California and is running that business, called Pasturebird. It's growing chickens in totally open pasture, in a mobile coop, with a roof over them for protection from predators. We don't know what the economics are. Are consumers going to pay so much more for an attribute? I have a gut feeling that whether Pasturebird is a great product or if it really helps us move forward on our taste initiative for everything else, I want to get into it.

There are people doing it, but can we do it on a large scale and make it profitable? We're willing to take a look. We always want to be a learning organization. That's one thing I stressed when I was CEO: if we find out something's different, we've got to find out why and pursue it. That's an important attribute of any company, to be a learning organization.

You mentioned Leah Garces from Compassion in World Farming. She was instrumental in the *New York Times* exposé written by Nicholas Kristof accusing Perdue of abusing chickens. From the outside, it seemed like that piece was a pivot point for the company. Was that true?

The Kristof piece did not influence us as to what we should or shouldn't be doing. Again, it's the consumer. They're the ones that pay the money, not a journalist doing an article.

When that piece came out, we could've said they were trespassing. They shouldn't have been on the property, et cetera, but one of the four pillars of our animal care program is trust, which means transparency: "Hey, open everything up. We have nothing to hide!" Consumers want to know how you raise your chickens, what you feed them, and they have a ton of questions around that, so I think transparency is super important.

Mark McKay [president of Perdue Premium Poultry and Meats] said, "Did we know that these chickens were looking like this?" and we said, "Well, no." Mark said, "We should call Leah's organization and thank them," and we went, "What? No!" While we didn't do that, we did say, "We're doing a lot of interesting things right now with different ways to grow chickens. Maybe you'd like to come up and see what we're doing."

That became the very first Animal Care Summit, with three [activist] groups, and it was very contentious. They were not happy with us. But then, as they saw some of the things we were doing, we developed some trust. After about the third Animal Care Summit, Leah called and said, "Compassion in World Farming is having our world meeting in London. I'd like you to come and be on stage with me to talk about what we've been through."

I said, "Is it safe?"

I was interviewed in London by Maryn McKenna, who wrote a book on antibiotics in animals [*Big Chicken: The Incredible Story of How Antibiotics Created Modern Agriculture and Changed the Way the World Eats*]. She was happy with us because we were the ones that caused the industry to go "no antibiotics ever." Leah and I were on stage, just the two of us, in a session called "Can a Large Ag Company and an Advocacy Group Develop Trust?" It was fascinating.

Because we're transparent, the animal welfare groups know what we're doing. We're telling them what we're going to do, and then we follow up and say, "This is what we've accomplished and what we haven't accomplished, but we're on a journey."

Being transparent is scary for some companies.

It takes leadership to convince the rank and file this is the right thing to do. Everything has been a closed book. When you're raising 13 million chickens a week, you know things are going to happen, going to go wrong. You're going to have a Craig Watts [the farmer quoted in the Kristof story] situation. We had to let him go, because he was not raising chickens the way we wanted them to be raised.

You're going to run into those situations. It's how you handle them. So, we've got mechanisms in place, even with some of the animal advocacy groups. We go to them and say, "Look, we just had this animal welfare situation. What do you think?" They give us their opinion.

They actually have some good ideas too! We came out with a product called Chicken Plus: it's chicken nuggets that have a serving of vegetables within the serving of chicken. That was an idea from Josh at the Humane Society of the United States (HSUS) [Josh Balk, then vice president of farm animal protection]. It was his idea to not go all the way to a pure vegan option, but to a flexitarian option. Somebody who wants to eat a little less meat but doesn't want to do away with meat.

It was the fastest introduction, got more ACV [all-commodity volume, a measure of product availability often used to determine the success of a product launch] than any product we ever came out with. It really came from the animal welfare groups' ideas.

So, you need to be open to anything. Don't close yourself off. There are good ideas out there. And you know, trust is an interesting thing. It's hard to come by, but once you have trust with somebody, it's valuable.

Remember, consumers understand that you're going to make mistakes. As long as you own up to them and say, "We're going to do something different as a result," they're a forgiving group.

Picking Battles by Listening to Your Customers—and the Socialists

ERNIE FARLEY
Partner, Good Farms

At first glance, Ernie Farley seems like a pretty typical agriculture executive. After earning a plant science degree from the University of California at Davis, he worked his way up to CEO of Coastal Berry, a large strawberry-growing operation, before striking out to form Sundance Berry, which he and his partner eventually merged with Andrew & Williamson Fresh Produce to create a multinational berry and tomato company.

The retail name of his company, Good Farms, reflects Ernie's desire to differentiate his operations from the stereotypical image of big ag as reckless overconsumers of environmental and human resources. He's both kind-hearted and capitalizing, willing to take a risk on forging an authentic relationship with anyone to improve the lives of his team and, in doing so, bolster his business. He doesn't care if it looks like he's losing—he's always got a bigger picture he's working toward, which includes making things better for farmworkers.

Over time, Ernie has managed to forge an effective partnership with labor unions, get closer to his largest customer, and improve the health and well-being of farmworkers, the environment, and the quality and safety of fresh produce. He even became president of the Equitable Food Initiative (EFI) board.

Ernie continues to insist on radical change. In one EFI meeting, he declared, "If this is just about bathroom breaks, shade, and clean water, I'm outta here," even though those are all things that farmworkers have had to fight to get. He wants to do more. That's certainly not typical.

Why did you take the risk to work alongside the labor unions and become a founding member of EFI?

Our largest customer—not the category buyer but the highest leadership in our part of the business—was encouraging it personally. It was the personal involvement of Jeff Lyons [then senior VP of fresh foods, Costco Wholesale] that pushed us. When he was engaged in EFI personally, that was a signal to us.

Of course, you want to do the right thing to improve things for your workers, but you weigh the business risks of trying. You've got to pay for your kids to go to school and for employees' salaries, so you've got to be smart about how you position your business. When suddenly somebody at that level was saying, "Well, you're going to get access to me," that was a huge carrot for us.

It still scared the shit out of us though. These people [the farm labor unions] can do a lot of damage to our business and our brand. I didn't even want them knowing who I am, let alone sit in a room with them.

We were risk-takers, but we weren't saints. We had an absolute agenda. It could have gone the other way, which it still does a lot of times. We have work stoppages probably more than our competitors because we talk more to our workforce than others. But climbing in bed with customers to solve social ills is a smart business move.

What was your relationship with the United Farm Workers (UFW) and the other labor advocates like before this experience?

If you ask Artie Rodriguez, the president of the UFW at the time, which grower had had him arrested more than anybody, I'm pretty sure he would have said me. Our battles made the *New York Times*, the *Chicago Tribune*, and the *Wall Street Journal*. We were a major target for the UFW. There were decades of distrust. "Hatred" is probably too strong a word, but "distrust" is not strong enough.

Working together to form EFI allowed us to listen to the other side of the debate. The format of a multistakeholder group brings a unique opportunity to see the social ill of labor abuses from other people's point of view, one that I never could've afforded before that. And I think the other way too, for labor groups to see our perspective.

Aside from getting brownie points with Costco, did transforming the relationship with the UFW and others make a difference in your business?

Yes. In March of 2015, there was major labor and civil unrest in the San Quintín valley of Baja, a major berry-producing region for North America. There were a lot of issues, but it was mostly about working conditions and some health-care issues. There were also *jornaleros*, day workers, who were getting paid in cash, and that led to all sorts of unhealthy working conditions, skirting rules, and those kinds of things.

I remember we said, "What should we do?" and we had a conference call; someone said, "We gotta have a barbecue." No, seriously. The roads are blocked, people are throwing rocks at trucks, the workforce can't get to work, and we were like, "Let's get the UFW guys. Let's get Peter [Peter O'Driscoll, executive director, EFI]. Let's get Costco. Let's go down there and have a barbecue. Let's disperse ourselves among the tables, and talk and hear and listen. Let's interact."

There were lots of multinational corporations involved there, and once this labor and civil unrest started, all the corporations got their people out. And we flew in. We had enough relationship capital. Now it was time to talk.

What do you mean by "relationship capital"? Who did you build capital with?

I say that [laughs] it's the socialists, which I say with humor, but there is an industry of people who advocate for worker and human rights. We didn't really have a relationship with those people in San Quintín. But the folks that came with us—my socialist friends who I'd worked with for years at EFI—did, and *they* had a relationship with *us*, so that solved everything. The groups in San Quintín came into the room with a different attitude.

Because we had put deposits in the relationship bank with people who were in that industry, we were able to withdraw from that bank account by saying, "We need you guys to come with us because we're concerned, but we'll never get an audience with the people that are doing this unless you're there."

We all struggled because of the civil unrest, but our operations did not suffer a tiny percentage compared to our competitors. Rather than hiding from the unrest, we were announcing who we were. It was a huge difference.

When you moved beyond Costco, how did you identify other buyers that would value your investment in EFI certification?

We learned quickly when trying to make a major change to get support from someone on the buying side with a lot of strategic power, not tactical power. A "head of buying" couldn't do us any good. It had to be somebody higher, and it couldn't just be a statement from them. This individual needed to stay personally engaged and empower people to stay in the process. If it was just words, the company wouldn't do shit.

You're a perfect example. Had you not just relentlessly said, "Well, how come this person's not answering their phone?" "Well, I don't understand why we can't" within your own organization, things would've been dropped. Nothing would've moved forward. Same thing in Walmart. There was a guy who was obviously empowered to be the person to stay in the trenches. You need someone to push the roadblocks out of the way, get the excuses out of the way. Someone with support from the folks way up the food chain. If not, after the initial rah-rah meeting, it's so easy for everybody to go away and do their day job. Because both the buyers and sellers have a day job—and it's not solving societal ills.

If you're relying on that one engaged, powerful individual, what do you do if they leave?

Buyers change jobs. Emotionally moving stories are neat, but they only last so long. I wish we had gone earlier to quantitative analysis. We are now, and we can prove that these changes in labor practices result in higher quality and less shrink [spoiled product], so our products are cheaper for our customers. As opposed to, "Oh, look, we made this person's life good." Yeah, we did that, but also you can go to your boss, because you're a buyer, and say, "I did pay more. But look, here's this quantitative information that says overall, it was cheaper. Look at the total cost, not just the price."

If someone says, "I'm going to pay you guys $1 more per box because I'm going to get this intangible thing called 'supply chain security,'" that sticks out because it's indefensible. Their boss comes at the end of the quarter and says, "Explain to me why this one supplier is getting paid $1 more." The answer can't be "What about our corporate thing about social change?" if their boss is hammering them on price. Why would I ever want to put myself in the position of saying, "Oh no, the buyer that paid me more for this thing is not going to get their quarterly bonus"? When the incentives aren't aligned, you can be "right," but real change won't happen.

Now, if you've got data, it doesn't really matter if people leave or bosses ask questions, and you have to tell the story again. Data gives you the Cliffs Notes version.

You have to learn to read your customer.

The inherent social ills are real and apparent to a smart, thoughtful businessperson, but going it alone is super dangerous and really a fool's errand. Striking when a customer sees a need as well can be a successful venture, though. Sometimes it looks like someone with power really supports this, not just chin music, not just "we're going to go to our annual meeting and say these things are really important to us." But then when you meet with them, they just say, "Here's our person from compliance."

But if the person who has a lot of power really stays involved and has people working for them who want to make sure this happens because the big guy or gal isn't walking away from this, that's "Jump on it!" because it pays huge dividends. It solves a problem that, as a businessperson, I want to solve but I can't do on my own.

If I woke up tomorrow morning and said, "Well, I'm going to solve the plastic problem by changing all the packaging on Good Farms. OK!", that's a fool's errand. There will still be millions of pieces of plastic out there on other farms, and if my customers and suppliers are not involved, and all the advocacy groups that are trying to change policy aren't there, I am all by myself. I'm not going to make a dent. Do I think that we have a plastics issue we've got to figure out? Sure. We can wake up tomorrow morning and blow a bunch of money on it to make a point, but as a businessperson, that's not a very smart thing to do.

If you're an intelligent businessperson, you know there are social ills in the system and you want to participate in trying to fix them. You just don't want to be alone, because you know that's not going to be energy well-spent. When opportunities form to make it possible that this ill could be handled in a different way, a thoughtful, smart businessperson should at least research the opportunity.

Lesson Two

How to Make Sustainability Your Mission (Literally)

"Maybe we should rewrite the Dream" might be the most audacious thing I ever said to my boss, cofounder and CEO Fedele Bauccio—and in thirty years of working for him, I've said a lot.

Fedele had tasked me with putting together our "corporate social responsibility platform," which may sound routine now, but this was 2004, and the term "CSR" wasn't yet in the American business lexicon, never mind sustainability. He kept saying, "I don't want it over here" (picture a passionate CEO showing his Italian roots by gesticulating in the air to his right); "I want it everywhere!" (arms circling as if he were doing the butterfly stroke).

What he meant was that he didn't want our values-based actions to be a marketing program tied only to philanthropy, an aside, or an afterthought. He wanted social responsibility to touch everything we did as a company.

To communicate that message to every Bon Appétit chef and manager, to all our clients and customers, to vendors, to *everyone*, as he wanted, I posited that to put it at the heart of our brand, we had to make it part of our mission, literally integrate it into the mission statement, or as it's called at Bon Appétit, "the Dream."

When Fedele founded Bon Appétit in 1987, he wrote a dream rather than a mission statement because he wanted people to make an emotional connection to the company. He wanted to inspire people to think bigger than they ever had before about what food service could be. He wanted everyone to imagine a type of company that didn't yet exist. (Read more about Fedele's approach to disrupting a mature marketplace in our interview on page 73.)

When founding his company, he wrote: "Our dream is to be the premier food service company known for its culinary expertise and outstanding customer service."

By today's standards, Fedele's dream isn't revolutionary, but it was when he penned it. This was a time when college and corporate food service consisted of cafeteria steam tables filled with mystery meat and soggy green beans. Fedele dreamed of real chefs cooking restaurant-quality food from scratch. He dreamed of roasting bones for soup stock, mashing real potatoes, and smelling the aroma of cookies baking.

So for me to tell this man that it was time to rewrite the dream—*his* dream—was somewhat radical—maybe even foolhardy. I was telling the man who transformed an industry that the time had come to scrap that. That the market differentiation he created when founding the company was no longer unique enough. While his dream had served us well for almost twenty years, it no longer encompassed all that the company could stand for.

To his credit, and to my relief, Fedele did not cling to his dream and what had worked in the past. He did not see me as someone who wanted to undo his life's legacy. Fedele was ready to take a leap again. So we worked on creating a new dream, a new vision for what food service could be. In the end, this was how we rewrote the dream:

> Our Dream is to be the premier onsite restaurant company
> known for its culinary expertise and commitment to socially

responsible practices. We are a culture driven to create food that is alive with flavor and nutrition, prepared from scratch using authentic ingredients. We do this in a socially responsible manner for the well-being of our guests, communities, and the environment.

From that point forward, everyone connected to Bon Appétit knew we were serious about the impacts of our food choices. Every decision we made was tested against that promise.

We began weaving our dream into the daily lives of our team members, starting with a national road show. We traveled to every region we served to look our chefs and managers in the eye and tell them about the new dream. We gave out framed copies, posted it in kitchens, and put it front and center in the employee handbook. Social responsibility was everywhere.

The thousands of Bon Appétit employees became the keepers of the dream. At one regional chefs' meeting, unhappy about a suggestion to switch seafood vendors to a company seen as having fewer sustainable options, a chef stood up and passionately recited the dream as his argument against the change. He was right. Even though there would've been cost savings, we kept our original vendor. While visiting a corporate account in Arizona, I was serenaded by two cooks who had turned the dream into a rap. They stood in the dry-storage room and spit the words out as lyrics, while the rest of their team bobbed their heads to keep the rhythm. Our dream had gotten into people's hearts—and into the heart of the brand.

At this point, when sustainability became central to our company's mission, our marketing materials also started to refocus to match. Before rewriting our dream, we had a menu sticker indicating that a dish was made with ingredients from a local vendor and a few other paltry indications of the care that went into sourcing our food. After rewriting our purpose, every campaign we created focused on words from the new dream (e.g., well-being, communities, environment, etc.) and carried a new gravitas. These weren't fads we'd seen on a

"This Year's Hottest Business Trends" list. These were the tenets on which our company was centered. We wouldn't abandon these ideals in favor of another trend. The dream was fundamentally who we were as a company. The dream *was* our brand.

Writing an authentic dream for your company or department requires defining your goals, values, and commitments. By aligning your words with your actions and weaving sustainability into your culture, you create a mission that not only shapes your company's identity but also impacts your brand's reputation, making it stand out in the eyes of customers. When it comes to your mission statement, you have to pull a Michael Phelps–level butterfly: write your dream, work hard to make it happen, and put it everywhere, or you run the risk of looking like you're just chasing a trend.

You may be wondering why lesson one wasn't to make sustainability your mission. It seems like the natural starting point would be a great, inspirational statement of purpose. I believe, however, that you need to pick the issues you're solving before you know your mission. When you know what you want to accomplish, you can then dream of that sustainable future.

How to Write *Your* Dream: Ask Yourself the Tough Questions and Be Honest

Note that I said to Fedele, "*Maybe* we should rewrite the dream." That "maybe" was pregnant with a tough question: How serious are you about wanting sustainability everywhere? Before you go and tear up your mission statement and start from scratch with a focus on sustainability, ask yourself that same question. Define where sustainability fits within your brand. Sustainability is not an all-or-nothing endeavor, so be honest with yourself about whether it's at the heart of your goals as a company. You may desire to make responsible choices when it comes to your company's practices—and you should, regardless of your ability to market those actions to your customers—but perhaps your company's focus is on being the most convenient, or the healthiest, or the most affordable, and not centered on sustainability.

This practice is not only important for executives who have the power to determine the company's mission statement. If your dream is indeed to create a sustainable company—or just to work for one— remember that we all have power. Writing your dream is an important step for middle managers, and even those just starting out, who also have a massive amount of power to make a positive impact. If you're not in the position to change the mission of your entire company, write your dream for your department or just for yourself. Look at what you control and imagine doing it in a more sustainable way, even if no one above you asked you to do so. A small, specific act, like a barista deciding to offer oat milk first before cow's milk or to compost coffee grounds, can be more important than a broad promise. Ask yourself where sustainability fits within your objectives as a company or as an individual, and then get to work writing that truth into your mission. At the end of the day, it's *your* dream.

Baked-in versus Half-Baked: Define Your Mission with Authenticity

Customers can sense your commitment or lack thereof to the issues that matter to them. If your goal is to create market differentiation based on your company's values, you'd better have those values baked into your company's dream. When I compare companies founded around the same time that sell similar products, the mission and vision statements of companies known for sustainability versus those of their competitors demonstrate the impact of a focused and authentic mission statement. While the latter may attempt to keep pace with rising customer interest in sustainability, their efforts aren't as impactful because they're ancillary to the brand.

The restaurant chain perhaps best known for its ethical sourcing, Chipotle Mexican Grill was founded in 1993 in Denver with the mission "to provide 'Food with Integrity'" and a vision "to do more than just rolling burritos while working to cultivate a better world."[1] Chipotle's in-store messaging, billboards, and much hallowed short film (which used Willie Nelson's voice, Coldplay's "The Scientist," and stop-frame animation to tell the story of factory farming) all come across as authentic, because they speak to the very heart of the company. (See my interview with Chipotle's former communications director Chris Arnold, page 220.)

On the other hand, another customize-your-own-burrito chain, QDOBA, which also started in Denver just two years later, chose a mission "to deliver flavors that make every occasion a celebration" and promised "an experience that delivers on new creations, old classics, and the ability to create your own masterpiece."[2] Their Clean Label Pledge and Responsible Sourcing promise come off as afterthoughts at best. As a result, Chipotle boasts a stronger brand association with sustainable practices, all starting with its mission.

Dreams that bake sustainability into the business don't all have to address the same parts of the broader sustainability challenge, either. While on a road trip in 2005, a San Francisco–based couple was disappointed by the dearth of good, fast-casual food choices. A year later they opened the first MIXT with a mission "to make it easy for guests to enjoy a delicious, high-quality, seasonal, and nutrient-rich meal."[3] Across the country in Washington, DC, in 2007, three college friends lamenting the same problem came up with Sweetgreen, but their mission was focused on "building healthier communities by connecting people to real food."[4] Both companies have strong, sustainability-focused ideals and commitments to high sourcing standards, but MIXT's are presented as being in the service of personal health, while Sweetgreen's speak to a larger social purpose.

I doubt most customers have taken the time to read the mission and vision statements of these companies, but I believe they can somehow sense the differences. There are dozens of indicators of a company's focus that flow from the mission. Menu descriptors, signage, organization of the website, conferences that executives speak at, content of employee training programs—they all are products of what leadership is dreaming about. Both Chipotle and Sweetgreen show the ability of a company's mission statement to impact the perception of a brand. The companies whose brand became synonymous with the eco-friendly food movement had their sustainability goals written right into their mission.

If your goal is to be known as a sustainable company, the first step is to weave it into your company's culture with a sustainability-focused dream.

Back, Back, Back It Up: Align Your Actions with Your Words

To be clear, rewriting your mission statement to include sustainability will only make a difference to your brand if you also align your actions with the new vision, not just your marketing. You can't fake this. It has to be a cultural reality so ingrained that people behave in ways that support the dream without even thinking about it. It has to be so ingrained that the choice to go with a higher-cost supplier *makes business sense* to you because it supports the mission.

When we rewrote the dream, our chefs had been sourcing locally for five years, we'd already committed to sustainable seafood, and our thinking about the connection between personal, environmental, and community health was already maturing. The revision I proposed was to keep our mission statement in step with our *operations*, not to change the direction of the company.

Conversely, in 2020, the Kraft Heinz Company announced what it called a strategic transformation with redefined values and a new vision: "To sustainably grow by delighting more consumers globally."[5] "Sustainably" was positioned as having a double meaning of perpetual financial stability as well as environmental and health impacts. This may have weakened the statement in the eyes of advocates. It's like the company was saying that sustainability matters *only* if it leads to growth and customers like it. Coupled with their proof points being forward-looking pledges rather than evidence of their existing achievements, the jury is still out on whether Kraft Heinz's commitment to sustainability is real and deep enough to weather economic downturns and stand true even if the term falls out of favor with customers. (There's nothing like a bad economy to send companies on the retreat from sustainability.)

With 150 years of brand reputation to contend with, Heinz's promises for a more sustainable future probably won't change the public's perceptions today. Miguel Patricio, chief executive officer at Kraft Heinz, admitted that this is a change in direction and that it was about what's to come: "This new ESG strategy reflects a new company value: *We do the right thing.* We're actively working each day to create a company and products we and the world can be proud of."[6] Articulating a new set of values, dreaming a new dream, is fantastic. It's what we need all companies to do if we're going to stop climate change and create a healthier food system, but just changing a mission statement isn't enough to erase perceptions about companies that build up over time. It's the behavior that follows the new words that will matter.

Hopefully the new mission signals a new culture and will change Kraft Heinz's impact on our world. For now, though, externally, the brand has not been transformed.

Customers are smart. There's a fine line between an aspirational goal and an empty promise, and people can sense the difference. Whether you're writing or rewriting your dream, being able to back it up with action is critical.

Incentives Matter: Align Your Systems with Your Mission

Having a mission statement that centers sustainability will create brand equity only if your purpose permeates all levels of your company. If your leader's vision is out of alignment with your daily practices, then it's worth no more than the virgin paper it's written on.

The sexy parts of building a brand around sustainability are the bold, inspirational statements you can put on the walls and in your commercials. For us, there are pretty pictures of farm-fresh produce. The critical components of authenticity, however, are the less photoworthy policies that customers may never even see, such as a performance appraisal and compensation strategy, and other internal success metrics. As a founding board member of EFI, a multistakeholder organization bringing together growers, farmworkers, retailers, and consumers to transform agriculture and improve the lives of farmworkers, I've seen repeatedly what happens when aspirations aren't buffered by systems redesign. The damage this disconnect does isn't pretty.

We'd meet with a top executive at a grocery chain or food-service company; they'd agree that the EFI approach would reduce risk in their supply chain and instruct their buying team to support the certification. A meeting with a semi-interested produce category manager would quickly follow. Then, nothing: no new purchase orders for EFI-certified growers, no bonus back to the farmworkers, no real change.

Getting the agreement of the company leader did not equate to action because, while the mind of the CEO had been changed, the policies of the company hadn't. The buying team members were still incentivized to purchase from contracted suppliers. Their departmental and personal performance was evaluated on their ability to garner cost savings. Nowhere did their key performance indicators (KPIs) reward them for making EFI-certified purchases. The company's ideals were out of sync with their administrative procedures.

The success of your dream and the success of your employees should be interchangeable. To truly embody a mission centered on sustainability, it's crucial not only to tout sustainable practices but also to ensure they are reflected in the performance metrics and incentivization strategies of your team.

At Bon Appétit, we created a numerical score based on a café's adherence to our sustainability commitments. Scoring above 90 percent made an employee eligible for company awards, like Manager of the Year, and the score was factored into employee bonus calculations. This step was straightforward, but one many companies don't take after they declare their commitment to sustainability.

At a large food company, Roma McCaig wrote carbon-reduction targets into the performance appraisals of each facility's engineering team. "Within their plan, they had to build out what the actions are and what it's going to take to ensure they hit that target," she told me. "We also moved all of the reporting to cascade down to the site level. We put in a common system, but everybody owned their piece of that data and could feed directly into that system. Then it was part of their performance evaluation."

You can start to see how progress toward sustainability requires directed effort and some real change in how you operate. Much of it is things you've done in other parts of the business and will be familiar. When you want to grow a market, you incentivize people to get new customers there. When you want to enter a new business sector, you build systems that will support it. This is no different. Sustainability, like any business challenge, is very much an operations challenge. So direct effort there. Don't assume that the dream will manifest itself. Make it happen.

Put Your Dream Everywhere

To make a mission that integrates sustainability meaningful, it must be *everywhere*. "Everywhere" looks like recruiting ads that highlight your company's commitment to sustainability, to attract people who share your values; measurable KPIs related to sustainability that are included in all job descriptions; internal corporate communications that feature stories of sustainability in practice at the company; and every salaried person having some part of their compensation tied to their success in making your mission a reality. You may have thought it was corny when I told you our frontline workers were rapping about our dream, but if you see something like that, you're doing it right.

At Bon Appétit, everyone knows that if you want brownie points with the leaders, tell us a story about the local farmer who grew the arugula that spices up today's salad special. We're just as interested in the student field trip you led to the ranch that supplies the café's beef as in a cost-saving change made to a schedule or repricing of a menu. Those at Bon Appétit who make the dream come to life are rewarded in both soft power and financial compensation.

Tie the success of your dream to the success of your company and the success of your people, and the power of your brand will follow.

ACTION ITEMS

How to Make Sustainability Your Mission (Literally)

If you want sustainability to be central to your brand, it must be part of your mission, not an afterthought or marketing initiative. You should weave sustainability throughout your culture, and your mission statement should accurately reflect your company's ethos, day-to-day actions, and long-term goals.

Here are key points to consider when thinking about how sustainability fits into your brand:

- **Ask yourself the tough questions.** Honestly assess whether sustainability is at the heart of your brand.

- **Define your mission.** Write a dream statement for what you have the power to change. Remember, even if sustainability is not a companywide objective, individuals at all levels can make a positive impact by incorporating sustainable practices within their own departments or roles.

- **If your goal is to create market differentiation based on sustainability, bake those values into the company mission.** A mission statement that directly and explicitly focuses on sustainability is necessary for sustainability to truly permeate the culture and create a strong brand association.

- **Back up your words with actions.** People can sense the difference between aspirational goals and empty promises. Ensure you are working every day to prove out your claims.

- **Align your systems with your mission.** Make your employees' success and your dream's success interchangeable. Incorporate sustainability initiatives into your team's performance metrics and incentivization strategies.

- **Put your dream everywhere.** Everything, from your recruiting ads to your job descriptions to your corporate newsletters, must tie back to the dream. This is how you build a sustainability-focused culture that will influence every decision at every level, from hourly employees to corporate executives.

The Dream as a Business Differentiator

FEDELE BAUCCIO

Cofounder and CEO, Bon Appétit Management Company

As I've heard him say on numerous occasions, Fedele Bauccio is "no Berkeley hippie," yet this straightlaced corporate executive has done more for creating a sustainable food system than most activists. Passionate and outspoken, Fedele reinvigorated the stale contract food-service industry by creating a unique brand in what was otherwise a commodity marketplace, with companies fighting to be the lowest-cost provider. He never shies away from taking a stand or loudly telling someone exactly what he thinks; he revels in being a contrarian.

As a result, Fedele has outlasted his peers and grown Bon Appétit to almost $2 billion in revenues. He's won awards from all sides, from recognizing his efforts against the unfair treatment of farmworkers, to Entrepreneur of the Year, to numerous lifetime achievement awards.

Much of what I share throughout this book comes from working alongside this visionary leader. I asked him to dig into the idea that his dream and his business—purpose and profit—aren't at odds.

Is changing the world a business opportunity?

In today's world, no company can succeed unless they define a purpose for what they're doing: "How do I make a difference and help make the world a better place? What kind of company do I have to create that's going to do that? What's the vision and what am I trying to accomplish?"

Look through a lens of what young people think about today, what they really care about. You'll see that the world needs to change because of climate change, how we're dealing with the environment, waste, and animal welfare, and that is a business opportunity! You'll start to think about what your purpose is and what you can create that's going to attract customers today and the future consumers of tomorrow.

So it's a differentiator?

I started in the contract food-service industry as a dishwasher in my college's cafeteria for Saga Corporation and worked my way up to divisional president. I then saw the need in the market, because even though there was lots of competition, the companies were all doing the same thing. Food was out of a box! There were no real chefs. It was a disgusting situation.

I felt we could do something different to separate ourselves from that group. I wanted to build a company on great food, cooked from scratch, no shortcuts, just the best ingredients bought fresh from people who cared about flavor. We would not be a commodity; we'd be special.

But you had to convince others, too.

I kept asking myself, "How do I inspire people to really change an industry, to do great food, and get the kind of quality that I really felt was needed?" For me, the answer was a "dream," a way to create an emotional connection.

This emotional attachment, this differentiation, not only inspired our own people and created an incredible culture but also inspired potential clients and customers. Telling that story, doing what I really believed from the very beginning about great food and sustainability, bringing in farmers with great products, was the right thing to do. It was so different. Nobody else was even thinking about that in the industry! That was a business opportunity!

How do you think about balancing doing the right thing and fiscal responsibility?

If you think about your purpose, then you will do the right thing. Tie a ribbon around that, tell the story, and you'll create a brand. I talk about our dream every single day. As long as I'm consistent in terms of what our dream is, what we're trying to create, then I know our people will do the right thing.

If we got that purpose right, we are aiming at what consumers care deeply about and the change they want to see, then we'll get more business and we'll be fiscally responsible. The bottom line will be there.

You've told me many times that "you can't cut costs to success." What do you mean by that?

I ran a restaurant concept called Stuart Anderson's Black Angus. We sold steaks for $4.95. Our food cost was well over 50 percent, yet we were very profitable. The light bulb went off in my head: it's all about revenues! If we can create more demand and more revenues by giving value to consumers, then it's not necessarily about the cost of food.

After that realization, I asked, "How do I create a company that builds revenues and focuses on the top line, versus cutting costs or looking at the bottom line?" Then I could be concerned only about quality, to drive frequency [how often a guest comes to your restaurant], or they call it "velocity" in grocery [number of units sold per distribution point]. How do I get people to return over and over? Maybe we never raise prices but create value, so we drive frequency and that leads to profitability.

How do you avoid raising prices when you're paying more for more-sustainable products?

Even if it costs us more to buy sustainable products, it's the right thing to do for the brand because it gives us the differentiation we need and a marketing tool to be able to tell a story that resonates with customers and potential customers. More people will come more often. We drive frequency. It doesn't matter if it costs more money if we can tell a story around it, that we're helping the community and the farmers by sourcing the best products closest to the kitchens, that nobody else can equal.

Have you accomplished what you wanted to in terms of sustainability?

Maybe we haven't gone far enough. We could have been stronger and more vocal about factory farms. We've tried, but we haven't solved the problems with chicken or beef production.

I once tried to put together a meeting of the heads of all the big meat companies to talk about change. We were going to create a roundtable and have the real decision-makers discuss what consumers wanted, what was best for our communities and the environment, what we could do better together. I was working with [then] Prince Charles, and we were even going to host the meeting at Highgrove House. No one showed up. The invitation came from Prince Charles, and nobody agreed to come! It was really sad.

I was saying, "If you create a more sustainable product for us, we're willing to pay more money." I knew I could get like-minded restaurant companies on board to buy this meat, too. This is a business opportunity. This is the future! They looked at me and said, "You're crazy!" Here we were willing to pay more money to do the right thing, and they don't want to change. They're the crazy ones.

At Bon Appétit we often made commitments without knowing how we were going to implement them. We've promised to buy products that didn't yet exist at a large scale. What's your thinking in taking that risk?

We made those commitments to *ourselves* because it gave us a road map to follow. We've always tried to push ourselves as a company, to be first and create initiatives that would help the brand and build differentiation. We drive ourselves and say, "We don't have all the answers, but this is what we're going to do. We're going to find the answers."

Can you think of a time when you wrestled with a sustainability choice because of the business implications?

No, not at all. I was convinced that dreaming of a more sustainable future was the right thing to do. And it made business sense. Maybe other people weren't convinced, but I was lucky because I had young, talented people around me, like you, who believed in what we were doing. And then it took off!

We started to speak publicly about trying to create a food system built on an ecological model, not just economics, and it created more benefit for the culture of the company. The culture of Bon Appétit is special. Our people, thousands of them, believe in the dream and believe that we are trying to change an industry. That is very important to me, the people of this company, and how they really have latched onto our sustainability initiatives and stayed with us for many, many years, because we are doing the right thing—or trying to do the right thing—for the future.

What advice would you give to somebody at a mature company who sees that the world is changing and wants to change?

It's really hard if what you are is cemented in consumers' minds. You need to figure out a new story that resonates with customers and create something unique. You almost have to start all over again. That probably means starting another brand. Keep the old brand but use the strength of the big company to launch a new direction. Use your infrastructure, your experience, and your capital to create something fresh. A little jewel of a company that can do things right.

What about a person who's a middle manager in a big company— can they make a difference?

They're well positioned to make change, in their *next* company. That's what I did. I spent twenty years with one company, understanding the industry, before I said to myself, "OK, now I know this industry like the back of my hand. I know exactly what I have to do to create differentiation."

A middle manager has an advantage because they've been there; they really understand the dynamics. People come right out of graduate school and want to disrupt everything. That's worked well in tech, but not in food. It really helps if you work in the industry for a while first, understand what it's all about, and then change it because you love it.

What would you tell a startup that wants to build sustainability into its brand?

I spend a lot of time with young entrepreneurs who want to change the world, and I keep telling them that the most important thing is taste. Whatever food product you're trying to create must taste great. If it doesn't, nothing else matters.

Then start small and focus consistently, day in and day out. Pick one or two things that you feel so strongly about that you can't sleep at night. So many young people try to do one thing and then five other things at the same time, and they don't know where they are. Bring it all down to one or two issues and focus on those alone.

After that, you've got to figure out a way to tell a story that creates differentiation. A dream. It's not just marketing; it's creating real uniqueness.

That's how you win, in my opinion. It's not easy!

Dream of Tackling Challenges

ROB MICHALAK

Former global director of social mission, Ben & Jerry's

Rob Michalak joined Ben & Jerry's as the ice cream company's PR czar in 1989, working alongside visionary founders Ben Cohen and Jerry Green-field. A unique opportunity to produce and cohost a magazine show for Vermont Public Television lured him away, but in 2006, a call from Ben & Jerry's presented an opportunity too good to pass up: a dream job, as the global director of social mission. The company had been acquired by Unilever, and upon his return, Rob helped reinvigorate the somewhat dormant social mission, taking on the values-driven supply chain; carbon reduction; sustainable agriculture for family-scale dairy farms; worker justice; diversity, equity, and inclusion; and much more.

Rob retired from Ben & Jerry's in 2020 but hasn't lost his appetite for facing challenging issues. He is not afraid of having tough conver-sations. Spurred by the murder of George Floyd, Rob and a group of fellow white men started to gather weekly over Zoom in an effort to understand their whiteness. They've continued to do so every Tues-day since. They call themselves White Men for Racial Justice and aim to use their place of privilege to dismantle structural racism. Ever the one to ask the confronting question, Rob asks, "Let's just cut to the chase. White men started this problem, created all the rules of the game, and the rules were all for us. So how are we going to be part of the solution?"

We spoke about instituting operational processes and systems to ensure that sustainability was integrated into the mission and the challenges of that.

The first time we met was at a Domestic Fair Trade Association meeting made up mostly of food co-op managers and small artisanal product companies who were trying to establish a high-bar standard for Fair Trade products produced in the United States and Canada. It was a reasonably radical group; one participant declared that only "100 percenters," meaning those completely dedicated to Fair Trade, should be allowed in the room. Ben & Jerry's wasn't 100 percent Fair Trade. Why were you there?

God bless him. He's got a right to say that everybody should be 100 percent Fair Trade. Part of my vision was to connect with the groups that were the most, what I would call, leading edge. The Domestic Fair Trade Association was made up of players who were really trying to work for a fairer, more equitable system. That's where we wanted to be, within that conversation, in that discussion.

The Unilever acquisition has been much lauded for preserving Ben & Jerry's commitment to sustainability. How was the spirit of the brand protected?

This was an unprecedented type of acquisition. Unilever and Ben & Jerry's board of directors, along with the cofounders, Ben and Jerry, worked out this legal document that established an independent board of directors for the social mission of the company that had legal authority. If they felt that Unilever was taking Ben & Jerry's off the social part of the three-part mission—product mission, economic mission, and social mission—they could bring legal action against Unilever.

Ben & Jerry's board has always been made up of independent people from activist organizations. When I left, we had the president and CEO of Heifer International, the executive director of Greenpeace USA, and the founder of the Oakland Institute, which is a very progressive human-rights think tank. You don't really find those kinds of board members on corporate boards. They would hold our feet to the fire by saying maybe we hadn't gone far enough, and we needed to hear better, see better, do better.

There were also mechanisms within the acquisition agreement to guide how, as the company grew economically and geographically, a formula would determine an increase in the social mission investment as well.

The social mission for Ben & Jerry's is part of its DNA. It's not a bolt-on, like "Well, let's think of something good to do." It's more like "OK, we're making ice cream. How can we source the sugar better? How can we source the dairy better? How can we build this stuff right into that product?" So it's part of the profit and loss; it's part of the success. It's part of the business model. It's not just a philanthropic thing, although we had a lot of philanthropy, too.

What investment in human resources was made to carry out the vision for growing the company's social mission?

We built this great team. When I went back to Ben & Jerry's in 2006, we were down to four people—the director's position, a part-time staffer in the United States, a full-time staffer who was doing sustainability work but was misassigned within the organizational structure, and another full-time person in Europe. We were able to build up from there. We got that sustainability person who was in the wrong reporting relationship onto our team. She worked with farmers, academics, and others to design a program within our dairy supply chain that was trying to work with these down-to-earth, hardworking Vermont family farms to see how we could start turning toward dairy agriculture that would have less impact on the environment and still be successful as a business. We also hired a full-time activism director, who led the social justice campaigns like supporting Black Lives Matter. We brought on a metrics person, because we were doing so much measuring and reporting with supply chain data, human resources data, Fair Trade reporting, climate reporting, and so on. And then we were able to expand and get an assistant manager for our activism manager, as those programs expanded both in the United States and then in Europe. The European team expanded, as did the teams in Asia, Australia, New Zealand, and so forth. As the company grows, it grows its social mission.

When I left, we had twenty-eight people who were directly associated with our social mission function, plus the marketing group, because a lot of this is really communications, marketing, social media and websites, and all that online stuff. There was a whole team in marketing that was dedicated to activist communications.

There was a *lot* of investment.

Did the approach to sustainability change at all postacquisition?

Before the acquisition, I think the culture was much more willing to take a risk and dive into stuff, which didn't always work but created novel scenarios, such as working with the Greyston Bakery in Yonkers, New York, an organization that has a no-questions-asked hiring policy. You just put your name down, go through the training, and you're hired. Greystone doesn't care about your past. They just care about you now and where you're headed.

We could have gotten brownies from anywhere, searched for the best price in the supply chain, but we got them specifically from Greyston Bakery because the more brownies we needed for ice cream, the more people they needed to hire to bake them.

When you're running a large supply chain, you usually don't look for small suppliers that could have redundancy issues, where if they go down, you don't know where you are going to get the brownies. A larger bakery would have all sorts of backup plans for delivering brownies, no matter what happens. But those were the kinds of risks we would take.

Now, on the other side of that equation, the thing that Unilever brought was this incredible, global organization that could help Ben & Jerry's both grow and expand things like our Fair Trade supply chain, which required sourcing from all over the world.

What was a risk you took that didn't pan out?

There was a different bakery that was hiring people returning to the community from incarceration. They produced apple pie for the American Apple Pie flavor that just never quite caught the fancy of the consumer. The flavor tanked and so did the bakery because they hadn't built a diversified business beyond Ben & Jerry's.

Unilever brought a certain discipline and rigor to thinking through decisions, so if we tried to work with a smaller supplier, how could we do that in a way that was safe for the supplier and also safe for the supply chain.

With all the good work you were doing, how did it feel when labor-rights groups launched the Milk with Dignity campaign, claiming workers at dairies supplying Ben & Jerry's were being mistreated?

That looked a lot different externally than internally. A group called Migrant Justice created the Milk with Dignity program and came to Ben & Jerry's to talk about the welfare of dairy workers. They wanted dairy workers to have a voice in a labor standard, much like the Coalition of Immokalee Workers had in Florida with tomatoes.

We thought, "Wow, OK, this is cool. This is 'on brand,' really on mission." At the first meeting, the group members said, "We're going to be working on a study of farmworkers. Are you willing to continue to meet on this?" We said, "Yeah," and so they went away to do their study. In the meantime, we were working on our Caring Dairy program that dealt with the animal, the earth, the farm owner, and the worker, which was in the pilot stage.

They came back for a second meeting with the results of their study. We saw it as, "Oh, you have a body of data that would be helpful for Ben & Jerry's to be able to improve its own program." But when Migrant Justice first came to Ben & Jerry's, we weren't hearing them right. And I'll be honest, we had several meetings, and they were saying one thing, but we were hearing another. They were saying, "We want you to do our program, not your program." Finally, after the third or fourth meeting, which meant several months had gone by, we got it and said, "Oh, OK, that's a different conversation. If we're going to have that conversation, we need to understand what the program is in detail."

At the time, they had a draft program. For success, we needed a program that the farmers could understand. So, there was a period of time when we were giving feedback about the economics and other structures related to the farms in an effort to get to something that would be possible to collaboratively execute. It took us a while to get there.

While this was all going on, they were campaigning, as they should be. What they were trying to do was create some pressure and noise to make sure that Ben & Jerry's didn't walk away from the table. But we never did; we were always at the table.

The public saw the campaigning and we saw it and heard it, but we were not going to say, "They're just throwing stones at a glass house." No, we thought, we haven't signed anything yet; let's honor that. They've got every right to say it, so we'll just keep working until we have something we can sign and something we want to say. We weren't the company that some people thought we were from listening to the protests, but I knew that, and it was OK. I said, "We'll get there," and we did.

The protests didn't concern you from a reputation standpoint or even personally hurt your feelings? We're all human.

No, I was working with an activist company. I knew that you have to have a thick skin, and because I had faith in the process, that it was going to arrive at a successful outcome. There was nothing to really be concerned or feel bad about.

Every once a while, sure, you think, "Oh, golly, another story," because you have to answer the media's phone calls. I would just say, "We're still talking," and not denigrate anyone, because this process was unprecedented with the voices of the workers at the table. It took us a little while to recognize it, but once we did, it was, "Well, this is really important.

Were there ever any issues that you got internal pushback on?

Definitely. I was part of a process. You have your whole leadership team, your CEO, the director of franchising, the director of sales, the directors of marketing, supply chain, and research and development, sitting around the table, discussing different issues. Then within the social mission group, the activism group would talk about what's coming up in the next year, which might be an election year or might involve an important UN Climate Change Conference.

We had discussions about what issues we were going to be tackling. A lot of times we focused on issues that had some relationship to our product, but then bigger issues came out, like Black Lives Matter. We were trying to understand what our position should be because the initial reaction of many corporate leaders was, "Well, don't all lives matter?" They didn't understand; we had to tune our ears—just as we'd had to with Migrant Justice to listen to the farmworkers—until we got it. White lives have always mattered. Black lives matter because of the way we're treating people and killing them! That was one of the more difficult positions to take publicly, because we did take a lot of heat on it, but what we found over the years was if we really stood for our values, it all worked out.

The Power of Aligning Teams and Systems

ROMA McCAIG

Former senior vice president of impact and communications, Clif Bar & Company

The romantic notion of a sustainability professional in the food industry is someone who gets to visit farms and walk fields all the time. The truth is, as Roma McCaig, former senior vice president of impact and communications for Clif Bar & Company, will tell you, most of us are as likely to be spending time with a project management Gantt chart as we are with a farmer. Lucky for her, Roma thrives on organizing and, more specifically, reorganizing. She's parlayed an understanding of business processes and a keen sense of organizational design into a career aligning sustainability goals with corporate strategy.

Prior to Clif, Roma was in corporate communications and rose to lead operations and continuous improvement efforts at a large food company. After a year, "responsible sourcing" was added to her job description.

So started Roma McCaig's career in sustainability, eventually bringing her to Clif Bar & Company, where she continued to use her superpower of helping sustainability efforts stay aligned with business goals, even when everything shifts around her.

When responsible procurement was dropped into your lap, where did you start?

Our company had made a lot of commitments across various aspects of corporate responsibility and sustainability, but specifically within sourcing around animal welfare, transparency, and human rights. But I saw that not much progress was being made, and every time we had to report, it was like an act of heroics to go collect all the data, because we hadn't built all these commitments into our operating model.

So I did what I had been doing with my strategy and operations role. I said, "This has to be integrated into our strategic planning process, into our annual operating plan. All the businesses need to know what their role is in this, what investments they need to make, and how it will affect their portfolio. Then we need to make sure that our processes, things like how we identify and qualify suppliers and how we track for reporting in these specific areas, need to be integrated into our systems."

I had to embed the commitments into our ways of working, starting with procurement, then extending into other aspects of supply chain and R&D.

Was senior leadership on board with this new focus on sustainability?

There were commitments around water reduction, waste reduction, and greenhouse gas emissions reduction. But then there was a reorganization and a new CEO and leadership team arrived, and these commitments were new to them, too. They hadn't been part of the vetting and decision-making process, and they wanted to know what the commitments were, where we were on them, and how we were going to achieve them.

There wasn't a lot of information I could share at the time. I felt like I was just in constant firefighting mode. If someone wanted to know why we're doing this, I had to dig up the history on it and figure out who all the different stakeholders we had to consider were.

So I put my communications hat on and said, "We're going to take a step back. We're going to understand what we're dealing with here. Let me do a little education before we start talking about the individual pieces."

First, I changed the language from "sustainability" to "ESG" [environmental, social, and governance] because I wanted it to be very clear that I was not the only person in the organization who owned this. I was the strategic partner and champion. I was going to shepherd and facilitate this, but it was owned by the entire company.

Next I said, "Here's why ESG matters: we are a publicly traded company; more than 70 percent of our institutional investors have signed on to the Principles for Responsible Investment [a UN-supported international network of financial institutions promoting sustainable investment], which means we are being evaluated on ESG risk within that investor portfolio." Basically, I said, "You need to care."

I looked at our ratings and rankings, and how we'd been performing over the years, and saw that we had been doing this climb year over year over year, then all of a sudden, we had hit a plateau. Why? Well, we were going up in the rankings when we were setting goals. We were getting a lot of credit for *communicating* goals, but then when we were asked where we were on the *progress* against those goals, performance plateaued. I thought we would start going downhill if we weren't able to show consistent progress.

That must have gotten everyone's attention. How did you then move to action?

I said, "Let's be aligned on the issue areas first, the areas of opportunity." I gave some specific criteria. One was our materiality assessment. What are the things that are most material to our organization as deemed by major stakeholders, both internal and external? Next, how are we performing on ratings and rankings? What did the raters and rankers care about? Third, what do we have in common with our peers? What issues are our peers focused on and where, if we locked arms together, could we drive change? Last, where are we already seen as a leader? Where do we have a strength that we want to take advantage of and build on? Where can we differentiate our company or one of our brands in particular?

With those criteria, the leadership team members landed on fourteen focus areas, spread across the E, the S, and the G, and said, "This is what we as a leadership team believe that we should be focusing on for the long term." Great, but you can't lead in fourteen areas. From that, they picked six to lead and eight to say we will never be seen as laggards. For example, community leadership was inherent to who we were, so that was an area we just wanted to build on. The key was we said, "The perception is that we're a leader. Now, what does it mean to be a leader?" The answer was moving from having goals that were activity-based to goals that were impact-based.

Where we wanted to make sure we weren't a laggard was animal welfare. We were not positioned to go above and beyond in that area because, in many cases, we were considered a secondary buyer, so it was more challenging for us to push the suppliers to move their practices in a certain direction. But we certainly could join the industry to push for that cause.

The word that comes to mind for all this is *systematic*.

We put all of that structure in place in order to have a very robust ESG plan that wasn't a separate thing that "Roma and her team" owned and ran. The entire business owned and ran it. Leaders would own a specific area, like nutrition, DEI, community action, packaging, climate action, animal welfare. There was a leader for each of the fourteen areas we had identified. I established a process, which was part of the company's larger strategic planning process, to build out a three-year plan for every one of those issue areas that included benchmarking to say, "Here's where we are today, here's where we are within our peers that, by the way, are the same peers that we use for financial benchmarking. Here are the commitments we would make if we wanted to be a leader. Here are the commitments we would make to stay on par. Here's what we need to do to make progress against those commitments over the next three years."

We followed that with a three-year rolling-forward plan. We got alignment on that and then went into the first fiscal year and said, "Here's how we're going to show progress. Here's all the investments we have to make, and here are the KPIs we have to hit." All of that was built into the respective functions and business units' plans for the year.

We also changed our accountability at the board level. Originally it was with the audit committee, and we moved to the governance committee because ESG was across the entire business. I was accountable to report to the board at least twice a year, first with the strategic plan and annual operating plan for the year, and then to report on our progress against commitments.

Can you give an example of the strategic plan being integrated into the company plan?

Think about greenhouse gas emissions reduction. Our company had so many facilities; we got our head of engineering on board as a key stakeholder and partner on our climate action plan. He managed a dedicated sustainability engineer who then worked to identify opportunities for reducing emissions. Well, that's great, but how are you going to actually get these things done? They had to identify a sustainability lead at every single site, and those people were given a target that they needed to hit every year. Within their plan, they had to build out the actions and how to ensure they hit that target. We put in a common reporting system, too. Everybody owned their piece of that data and could feed directly into that system. All this became part of their performance evaluation.

How do things differ at a company like Clif, where sustainability was part of the ethos from the start?

When I came to Clif, it had also gone through a major restructuring under a new CEO. I spent a lot of one-on-one time with team members understanding the company history. Clif wasn't new to things like sustainability. It had been doing it for twenty years. So, what was the opportunity?

I helped them focus. We outlined some key long-term commitments like Science Based Targets for our net zero commitment, signed on the 10X20X30 [an initiative bringing together 10+ of the world's largest food companies, each engaging at least twenty suppliers to halve food loss and waste by 2030] and the Ellen MacArthur Foundation goals for packaging sustainability, and we set some audacious goals for company donations, employee participation, and our employee service program, and so forth.

Was it hard to get people to give up their pet projects?

I again took it all to our leadership team and said, "Look, this is where we want to focus. Anything else we choose to do, if it doesn't align with this, why are we doing it? And by the way, we're focusing on this because it's in service to our company purpose, which is 'to redesign the business of food for the benefit of health, equity and Earth.' It's in service to our growth game plan, which is our 2030 strategy. And it's in service to our Five Aspirations business model, which says we're going to sustain our people, community, planet, brands, and business."

I also explained that if you're going to make these commitments, you're going to report on them. It's one thing to say, "Hey, we're going to do these things." It's another to show your progress.

Until August 2022, we were a family-owned private business, so we didn't have reporting requirements. Still, we made ten of our commitments public facing, and we reported our progress against those. The other commitments we kept internal until we felt like we had strong enough measurable targets in place, because we still had to design and figure out some of them.

I worked with every functional leader to make sure these things were built into their strategic plans. For example, sourcing. We have an organic goal, so delivering against that goal needs to be in the strategic plan and the annual operating plan for the sourcing team. With greenhouse gas emission reduction, that goal has to be in the supply chain operating plan and the bakeries' annual operating plan as well. We also have an annual bonus program that is designed around our Five Aspirations. We have targets for the planet, which are scope 1, scope 2, and scope 3 emission-reduction targets [the accepted protocol for measuring a company's direct and indirect greenhouse gas emissions], and we have targets for the community, which is participation in our employee community service program. When we hit those targets, contributions are made to the bonus payout to all employees. Everybody now has a stake in this.

You changed a lot of systems at both companies. At Clif, you also changed the attitude about publicity to an extent.

Clif had historically been humble, to its own detriment. People just didn't know it had been doing all these great things for so long. People at Clif said, "Wait a minute, why is that brand getting all the credit? We were already doing that. We were the first!" Well, because you don't want to talk about it. There was an attitude of "They should just know we do those things." But how were we going to let them know we do that? We changed.

The hard part about the marketing aspect is that it's really important for people to know about your commitments, but it also can seem like greenwashing to some consumers.

For your commitments to be authentic, they have to be integrated into your business practices. At Clif, we protected our planet for a lot of reasons. One of the big reasons is access to outdoor places so that people who enjoy Clif products can use those products when they're going for a hike or a bike ride. We also want our employees to be able to live those values at home. So, we provide an incentive every six years for employees to buy or lease electric cars. We provide an annual incentive of $1,000 for employees to green their homes, be it putting in a vegetable garden, energy-efficient appliances, all LED lights, a compost system; there's so many different things that you can do that make your home greener. Also, there's an incentive for employees to purchase a bicycle for commuting. Things like that show we're authentic because we're aligned as an organization.

What would you tell someone who's embarking on this sustainability journey at their company?

Start small. Fewer is better. If you can, really double down on just a few things. It's going to go a lot further in terms of the impact that you can make.

Really understand your business. A lot of classes and MBA students I talk to want to know, "How is my MBA going to help me in sustainability?" I say, "Well, you need to have really strong business acumen to be able to integrate sustainability into all aspects of the business, to explain why it matters, and to make a good case for it in the language of the person you're trying to sell it to."

Immerse yourself in the business. I tell that to new leaders. We were acquired in August 2022. New leaders are coming in from the parent company trying to understand what Clif is and what makes us special. It's like learning a foreign language. I've had six years of Spanish, and I'm still not fluent because I was never immersed. You have to go through an immersion to really understand the why and how it works.

How to Make Meaningful Change

"You don't *deserve* my melons," said Brett Grohsgal, defiantly. He was standing behind his Even' Star Farm product, literally, at a local farmers' market table in Maryland in 2004.

Brett was talking to Kimberly Triplett, an executive chef for a Bon Appétit university campus. After tasting the juicy, aromatic melons, she had attempted to place a very large order. She was excited: she located the flavorful product from the exact kind of local purveyor she had been assigned to find, and she was about to provide him with an unprecedented purchase. A huge business opportunity for Even' Star.

Or maybe not. "I put so much care into these melons," Brett told her, "I am not going to have them just sold into a college cafeteria."

Brett wasn't easily swayed, but thankfully, neither was Kimberly. As clear and direct as his sentiment was, Kimberly wanted those delicious, sweet melons and wouldn't take no for an answer.

So, she went out to see Brett at his farm and jumped through all the hoops he laid out for her, arriving early in the morning to walk the fields with him—barefoot, so as not to stomp on the seedlings.

She convinced him that she cared about those melons the same way he did.

In turn, she brought Brett to her university kitchen. As the whole culinary team eagerly sliced into his melons, Brett witnessed their appreciation for his fruit. The initially incredulous farmer said she could place an order after all.

Kimberly found herself at that market trying to woo Brett and earn the right to buy his melons because Bon Appétit had declared that we were going to favor local producers. We placed our highest value on supporting small farmers who were growing for flavor, not just for volume and efficiency. We weren't trying to just check a box saying we bought locally because it was a trendy thing to do. We were trying to meaningfully change the food system. We incentivized our team at every level to take the extra step to support small farmers.

To successfully build a brand on sustainability, you need to make meaningful change. That means going beyond what's already easy to do in the marketplace. You can't just hang back and watch what other companies do. You're going to have to act first, focus on a specific outcome, and run hard in service of making a positive impact for your community or the environment.

Fail to make meaningful change, and you're just a company chasing trends or, worse yet, risking the accusation of greenwashing. Figuring out which dynamics are at play and how to alter them, though, takes a lot of thought and intentional strategy. A chef buying some melons may not seem like a transformative act, but because Kimberly's work was part of a larger strategy that spoke to the very core of our business, it was revolutionary both for our brand and for the communities we serve. It was meaningful.

I've worked on countless cases like Kimberly and Brett's, some that succeeded and some that failed. But they've taught me to distill the path to meaningful change down to five steps. They apply to business both big and small in the food industry and beyond:

Step one: Find your purpose.

Step two: Find a leverage point.

Step three: Define your terms and parameters.

Step four: Set targets and measure.

Step five: Align all your systems to support success.

Let's take each in turn.

Step One: Find Your Purpose

As Lewis Carroll said, "If you don't know where you're going, any road will get you there." Understanding why, as an organization, you're setting a sustainability goal is necessary to ensuring you meet it. It will help you identify a path for success, understand when you've achieved it, and guide your decisions when you come to a crossroads.

Kimberly pursued Brett's melons so doggedly because we had laid out a very clear purpose: support small farmers who are growing food for flavor. In the late nineties, at Bon Appétit we had what we called "a crisis of flavor on the plate." Food just didn't taste the way food used to taste. If you grew up in New Jersey or California before farming was industrialized, maybe you remember picking a ripe, probably misshapen tomato and biting into it like an apple. The thin skin could barely contain the fruit's sweet juice.

Would you do that today with a supermarket tomato? Modern tomatoes are round but also flavorless and almost dry on the inside. As culinarians, we started to notice this in more and more foods. Think of a Red Delicious apple, the kind that has been part of school lunches for years. Red, yes. Delicious, no! What had happened to food? Where had the flavor gone?

We learned produce was being bred for travel, not taste or flavor. It was made to withstand long distances and sit on a shelf looking pretty. We found a study by Rich Pirog, then associate director of Iowa State University's Leopold Center for Sustainable Agriculture, that calculated the average distance food was traveling from farm to market in the United States was 1,500 miles. Everyone knows now that food is being shipped great distances, but put yourself back twenty years when Kimberly was at the farmers' market eating melons. The local sourcing concept wasn't a thing yet. Thinking about where food was being grown was an awakening for us. And it was the impetus for our first-of-its-kind, large-scale, local purchasing program, dubbed Farm to Fork.

We wanted the best-tasting food possible, so a small group of Bon Appétit executives set out to find it. Our director of culinary support and development said, "Oh, I know where there's a farm stand," and drove there, only to discover it was gone, paved over. I called a high school classmate who had taken over his family's farm; he said, "We grow leeks, leeks, lots of leeks." All they were growing was leeks. What happened to everything else? I like leeks, but it was hard to imagine filling one of our café menus with just leeks. These experiences reinforced the idea that food was not being grown to be the most delicious and interesting, but to be the most consistent and suited for transport. This needed to change.

We defined our purpose to support the type of food producers who were growing for flavor. That guided every parameter of our local purchasing strategy. Chefs were tasked with not just buying locally but looking for a particular *type* of farmer or rancher, one who cared as passionately about flavor as we did.

Our "why" wasn't about capitalizing on a trend, meeting consumer demand, or even about sustainability, really. Buying locally spoke to our very foundation, that original dream of Fedele's to be known for culinary expertise, of offering restaurant-quality food in an institutional setting.

Brett's blunt concerns about where his wonderful melons were going to wind up, whether the literal fruits of his labor were going to be truly valued, made him a more attractive partner—even though it meant Kimberly had to work a bit harder. Those melons were worth it, because they were the key to meeting a personal goal of Kimberly's (incentives) and a corporate value of Bon Appétit's.

Other companies have different purposes that drive their commitments. Gary Hirshberg has worked throughout his career at Stonyfield Organic yogurt to reduce chemical use. (Learn more about how that aim actually sparked the founding of the company in our interview on page 43.) Sometimes that purpose is obvious, like putting "organic" right in the name of the company and never bowing to pricing pressure to create a cheaper, nonorganic line.

In other cases, the goal to reduce chemical use may *appear* to take a back seat to other issues, like Gary's intense focus on GMO labeling. He even stepped down as CEO of Stonyfield to direct the Just Label It campaign. Gary's beef with GMOs isn't about the fundamental technology, though; it's about the way GMOs are commonly used, resulting in the skyrocketing growth of superweeds, requiring ever more herbicides. Over the sixteen years from 1996 to 2011, the use of GMO crops increased herbicide use by 527 million pounds. In addition to environmental impacts, herbicide overuse increases health risks for the communities surrounding farms. Researchers have linked exposure to these chemicals to reproductive problems, Parkinson's disease, and an elevated risk of non-Hodgkin's lymphoma.[1] Stemming those risks drives Gary's work. So it turns out Gary's campaign for GMO labeling has the same purpose as his commitment to organics: reducing chemical use.

Your purpose may have nothing to do with food. Horrified by the fact that 85 percent of all textiles wind up in landfills each year, you might be starting a clothing company with an aim to reduce the wasteful practices of fast fashion. That would probably mean focusing on higher-quality fabrics and more classic designs that will stand the test of time. To further your goal of reducing waste, you could also design a secondary line of garments that utilizes the scraps left over from cutting out the patterns for your primary line. Or you could develop technology that calculates how to use more of a single piece of raw fabric to reduce waste. Since your purpose is reducing waste, you might continue to use cotton because it's long wearing, even though cotton production is extremely water intensive.[2] Reducing water use is not your brand's principal purpose; keeping fabric from being thrown away is your focus.

If you and your team don't know your purpose and what exactly you're trying to achieve, how will you come up with your game plan? Whether your aim is greater flavor on the plate, fewer chemicals in the air and soil, or less waste, the first step to making a meaningful change is to define your purpose. Once your purpose is clear, you can begin scheming about how to accomplish it.

Step Two: Find a Leverage Point

A leverage point is the action you can take that catalyzes market transformation. Write the correct new policy, switch a critical supplier, or take a bold stand, and the result will be a new product introduced to the marketplace to meet your needs, production practices modified to be more environmentally or socially friendly as you've specified, or a blow to the popularity of an item produced in a destructive way because you've proven it's out of favor.

I discovered the power of our leverage when the head of NORPAC Foods, Oregon's largest food processing and packaging cooperative, came to our California offices to ask us to call off our boycott of their frozen vegetables—even though we'd only ever bought a few thousand dollars' worth of their product.

Bon Appétit had been the first company to sign on to a boycott led by the Northwest Treeplanters and Farmworkers United, better known by its Spanish acronym PCUN (Pineros y Campesinos Unidos del Noroeste), an independent farmworker organization. PCUN had smartly started drumming up support for their cause on college campuses. A student protest at Willamette University caught the attention of our team (as well as that of the representatives working in the Oregon State Capitol building, conveniently located across the street). At an ensuing meeting with our leader, Fedele, PCUN representatives shared photos of substandard farmworker housing. They recounted stories of worker intimidation on NORPAC member farms. Fedele was deeply moved. When he pulled the data on our purchases from NORPAC and saw how little we bought, joining the boycott was a no-brainer.

Since we were such a penny-ante customer, why did the NORPAC president care that he'd lost the sale of a few bags of frozen corn to us? The answer requires a bit of food business supply-chain inside baseball, but bear with me. Shelf space in a distribution warehouse, known as "slots," is precious. When we told our distributor we'd no longer accept NORPAC products, it was easier for them to switch to a competitor than to add a non-NORPAC option for just us. That is, instead of using two slots for frozen corn—one for the NORPAC product they'd always carried and one for the alternate product our chefs would buy— they just stopped stocking the NORPAC product altogether.

We'd gotten NORPAC kicked out of distribution. We had the power to make meaningful change for farmworkers. NORPAC felt the financial pain of the boycott and, eventually, came to the table to sign an agreement with PCUN. By changing our purchasing specs, we'd found our leverage.

Finding the right leverage isn't always that obvious. Combining good intentions with size isn't necessarily a formula for success. When we banded together with our parent company, Compass Group, to ask a large agricultural company to sell us what I termed "Imperfectly Delicious Produce," food that would otherwise have gone to waste because of cosmetic challenges or no clear use, we learned the potential downside of having leverage.

We visited a multi-vegetable-growing operation that held lucrative contracts with Compass Group. We walked the fields and toured processing plants to identify items destined for compost that we could instead use in our kitchens.

We had several big successes in saving vegetables from waste—or so we thought. The machine that turned heads of broccoli into precut florets created a pile of little bitty pieces of broccoli that had fallen off in the process. We dubbed those "broccoli fines" and had them bagged up; chefs loved tossing them into soups and stir-fries. Success! Cauliflower turns yellow when its leaves peel back in the fields and expose the white head to the sun. No change of taste, just a change of color. "Sunkissed cauliflower" was born, and those completely edible plants were now useful, as were the heads that had previously been seen as too big or too small. Success! We estimated we could increase the farmer's yield by 20 to 40 percent. We were on a roll.

Maybe our favorite "save" was clipped spinach. Spinach fields are harvested by a machine that cuts and collects all the mature leaves of a certain height. Greens don't all grow at the same rate, though, so the machine only harvests the very top of the shorter leaves. The trimmed spinach plants remained in the field, unharvested even after they grew, because with their clipped tops, they were considered damaged. Once our chefs chopped up or cooked these imperfectly good spinach leaves though, no one knew the tips had been clipped. These second-harvest greens represented a whopping 50 percent reduction in water usage and no additional fertilizer to grow. This was a fantastic environmental savings, and additional revenue for the farm!

At least that's how it seemed.

A couple of years into the Imperfectly Delicious Produce program, the person on our team in charge of negotiating and managing the fresh produce contracts left the company. The sales rep for the farm operation took that opportunity to confess that they were selling us the cases of second-cut spinach below cost. The expense of bringing the harvesting machine back to the field and of triple washing, boxing, and shipping the spinach exceeded the selling price. They were losing money every time we "rescued" those leaves, but they kept selling them to us to make a big customer happy. They knew how proud we were of the success of the program and wanted to keep bolstering this relationship, which was profitable on their other products. The second-cut spinach was a loss leader.

Losing money for the farm and getting a good deal were not the intents of the program. Our goal was to prove that harvesting cosmetically challenged produce was a win for the farmer and the environment. Our buying power had perverted that calculation. We'd unintentionally misused our leverage.

We offered to buy the second cuts at the same price as the perfect, first-cut spinach to continue to reduce water and fertilizer use, but the farm said that even at market price, they'd be losing money due to lower yields. So we removed the second-cut spinach from our Imperfectly Delicious Produce order guides, but we continued with the other products that the farm confirmed did make economic and environmental sense. And we implored them to believe that what would make us the happiest as a customer was honest information, not just a blanket yes to whatever we requested.

We had found our leverage but failed to ensure we were working toward our greater purpose: in this case, proving that it is environmentally and economically beneficial to harvest everything that is planted.

If you're an extremely large purchaser, you've got a lot of leverage and need to be conscious of how you're using it. Be careful that you're making a change that is sustainable over the long term, not forcing your suppliers or partners to placate you because of your outsize power in the market. Find your leverage and use it responsibly.

Step Three: Define Your Terms and Parameters

Once you establish your goal and you've found your point of leverage, ask yourself what is required to meet your expressed aim.

If, like Gary from Stonyfield Organic, your primary goal is to reduce chemical use, your terms might be to require organic certification; your parameters would extend to all purchases, including those from big ag. In this case, it's not about buying locally; it's about converting the largest amount of acreage to organic. To meet the goal, you must change the practices of producers everywhere.

Conversely, Bon Appétit's Farm to Fork purchasing program was about supporting small, local farmers. To set its terms and parameters, we first had to define what we meant by "local" and who we were talking about when we said "small farmers."

Since we were the first food-service company to craft a local purchasing policy, we had to define the basics of what local meant to us. After much discussion, we settled on our terms: local means 150 miles from a kitchen—a balance between close enough to be a reasonable day's drive for a farmer and far enough to account for large metropolitan areas where our downtown cafés might be far from farmland. Since then, 150 miles has become the de facto measurement of what constitutes local for most policies.

There are valid exceptions to that rule for purchasers aiming to support hyperlocal businesses; for example, the University of Chicago's UChicago Local initiative, which is aimed specifically at the South Side neighborhood and limited to nine nearby neighborhoods. However, I've seen policies that expand the parameters of local to a 450-mile radius. I'd argue that's a "regional" program. It may be important for other reasons, but it won't satisfy those who focus on having a truly local impact.

But for local-food advocates, the concept of local encapsulates much more than just a close geographic distance. After all, there could be an industrial farm with poor practices that's less than 150 miles away. So local also means supporting small producers who are good stewards of the land and members of the community.

To us and to those in the food movement, buying locally has always been about supporting small producers who are more likely to grow a diversity of products, including fragile heirloom varieties that don't ship well and thus have lost favor with big ag. Many of our Silicon Valley cafés were within 150 miles of the Salinas Valley, where giant agribusinesses grow almost half of the nation's lettuce, broccoli, and cauliflower. Even though those farms are technically nearby, they aren't the ones growing the delicate produce with a wide range of flavors that we were trying to protect.

Without the correctly defined terms, buying from these Salinas Valley farms would easily check a box for local purchasing. To control for this, we set the terms for what we meant by "small." The USDA defines a small farm as under $250,000 in gross annual sales and a "very large farm" as having revenues over $500,000.[3] Every local-food advocate we talked to disagreed with these cutoffs, pointing out that even a farm grossing $500,000 would struggle to support a family without an additional source of income. (On average, off-farm income contributed 82 percent of total income for all family farms in 2019.[4]) Taking into account the slim profit margins in food production, we set the gross revenue maximum for Farm to Fork vendors at $5 million annually. Those nearby Salinas Valley mega-farms would not qualify.

There hasn't been a generally accepted definition of scale, yet companies have gotten into hot water when they've clearly ignored the spirit of the food movement's desire to support "small." Aramark, another food-service company, was embarrassed by an exposé showing that they had met their contractual obligation to buy locally at the University of Kentucky by supporting a Coca-Cola bottler in Lexington.[5] The Washington, DC, restaurant Founding Farmers' misleading purchasing claims and undisclosed ties to big ag were called into question by the *Washington Post*, starting a years-long feud of sorts between the owner and restaurant critic Tom Sietsema.[6]

Both were checking boxes and trying to get credit for it without setting thoughtful terms to meet their goal. Not a good look. Be careful when defining your terms and setting your parameters. And be aware of the general consensus on what terms mean, or the spirit of a term's usage, before exploiting it. If you ask a hundred people on the street if buying from a Coca-Cola bottling plant supports local sourcing, most would scoff. Customers can tell when you're taking shortcuts or exploiting loopholes.

Our primary goal was to ensure the success of the farmer growing the flavorful food we desired, so we could keep buying it. So we set parameters that considered the farm's size and accounted for the unique circumstances of small producers. We did believe that healthy soil resulted in more flavor, so we homed in on farmers who were good stewards of the land. However, requiring a small farmer to do the requisite recordkeeping for organic certification, pay the certification fee, and tie their hands completely so they could never ever use pesticides or fungicides might be counter to ensuring their success, which would go against our goal.

A farmer in St. Louis once said to me, "I have one field. If I get a fungal outbreak, I need to be able to use a fungicide as an emergency measure. I can't afford to disc under [till back into the ground] an entire season's produce to maintain organic certification. If you want to know if I'm using pesticides, don't look for an organic sticker on my produce; look at this."

He showed me two pictures. One was of a bird's nest built under the plastic film he used to warm his crops and protect them from insects. A mother bird had tucked her babies under the black sheet for safety. A second photo showed his kids covered in mud. "Could a bird raise her young there if I was overusing chemicals? Would I let my kids roll head to toe in the dirt if it was full of pesticides?"

We decided that instead of requiring organic certification, we'd stipulate that Farm to Fork producers must be owner-operated. Our thinking was that if you were working the land yourself, you were less likely to overapply poisonous chemicals. This approach is imperfect, but it sets up terms and parameters that lean in favor of the farmer's success, which in turn serves our goal. We relied a fair amount on trusting these people, but they were people in our community, people we could get to know. Their reputations mattered to them since they live and sell in the same place. And they were putting their name on the product, not selling to an aggregator or marketing collective.

When you set your terms and parameters, don't focus on checking preexisting boxes. Focus on serving your larger goal and what meaningful change looks like in the real world.

Step Four: Set Your Targets and Measure

Setting targets seems straightforward, but there's an art to it (and it includes revisiting elementary school math). First, you've got to decide how you view failing to meet goals. Then, define exactly what and how you're measuring. Finally, always leave yourself a little wiggle room.

A year after setting a goal that 25 percent of the meat we bought at Bon Appétit would be certified by a high-bar animal welfare organization, I was caught off guard when purchasing manager Curt McClusick highlighted a disturbing calculation. "We're buying more humanely raised pork," he said, "but it's pushing us further away from our goal to buy humane-certified meat." To measure against our goal, we divided certified purchases by total purchases. We wanted the fraction to come out to one-fourth or better. Buying the humanely raised pork increased the bottom number because that meat cost more, but it didn't increase the numerator because it wasn't formally evaluated and certified by a credible third party, and that was our agreed-on metric. We could have said, "But it's more humanely raised," but that wasn't what we agreed to measure.

What did we do? We weren't hitting our goals, but we sort of were, too? Did we just say "close enough" or did we need to change our measurements somehow? This is why I always counsel businesses to think critically about what you're measuring and how, especially as you build incentives against hitting those targets.

There are three things you need to figure out with your measurements: your philosophy, your parameters, and your expectations.

Measurement Philosophy: Does Close Enough Equal Good Enough?

Before setting a goal, you need to pick a target-setting philosophy. You have two options, which are based on how your executive team views "failure."

Measurement philosophy one: Be reasonable. Set a reasonable target, work hard, get there, and show success.

Measurement philosophy two: Be audacious. Go for the big, hairy, audacious goal (BHAG, as coined by business-writing guru Jim Collins) that might be improbable to reach, work like hell to get there, make incredible progress, but fall short (for now), and still claim victory.

If you want to be seen as a groundbreaking industry leader, you've got to go with option two. Take on an issue no one else has touched yet (as Bon Appétit did with gestation-crate-free pork), commit to a higher percentage than anyone else has, or set a shorter implementation timeline. Be *bold*. The risk is undoubtedly bigger; if no one else has done it before, there's probably no clear path to success. Of course, the reward is bigger, too.

On the other hand, your aim might be to keep pace with the market. If that's the case, it's option one for you, but then be sure to hit all your goals, because falling short of a goal that others are reaching is much more damning than not meeting a BHAG that no one else has even set, much less accomplished.

In general, startups tend to choose option two, while older, more established companies take the more conservative approach. It's hard to turn a big ship, so incremental changes are more palatable to a large corporation that will need to rejigger massive and complex existing systems; find larger supplies of a new product, possibly even globally; and probably has a target on its back as advocacy groups are actively watching. There are exceptions, of course, that come from leadership. Ultimately, the approach you choose depends on the culture of your organization. Pick a goal based on your company's approach to hitting targets, level of ambition to be the front-runner, and stomach for failure. (Read about how Lisa Dyson learned the importance of a clear BHAG at her first startup and how that led her approach at Air Protein, in our interview on page 135.)

Measurement Parameters: Apples to Apples, or Are Oranges Included?

Defining what and how you're measuring to declare success for your goal sounds simple, but the math can get a little complicated, as we saw with the more ethically raised meat example that started this section.

Most sustainability commitments are a percentage of purchases, such as Compass Group's goal to buy 25 percent of its coffee from Fair Trade or eco-certified sources, or an absolute increase, like Chipotle's purchasing pledge to "increase pounds of organic, local, and/or regeneratively grown and raised food year over year."[7] Carbon commitments often combine a percentage-reduction target with an end goal of getting to net zero. For example, PepsiCo says, "We plan to reduce absolute direct operational Scope 1 and 2 emissions by 75% and our absolute indirect value chain emissions by 40% by 2030 (2015 baseline). In addition, we pledged to achieve net-zero emissions by 2040, one decade earlier than called for in the Paris Agreement."[8]

To calculate results, you'll create a fraction like we did with the pork: the numerator is the product you're buying that meets the commitment, and the denominator is the total amount you're buying. But what exactly are you measuring? How are you counting it—dollars? units? weight? And do you have the data? How precise is your accounting system?

Take Bon Appétit's commitment to local purchasing. We required chefs to spend 20 percent of their food budget with our registered Farm to Fork vendors. "Spend" clearly means that the unit of measurement is dollars, but "food" is less specific than it may appear. For example, we excluded beverages from our local purchasing calculation because we had specified "food." Other food-service companies such as Sodexo decided to exclude everything except *produce*; apparently they viewed the local-food movement as being about fruits and vegetables.[9] So when Sodexo says it tracks "percentage of local foods purchased," it means percentage of produce. The denominators are different between the two companies even though they may be stating the same commitment. One is "all food" and the other is just produce.

Measuring by spend is usually easiest because you have that data already. It's in all accounting systems. On the other hand, a valuable measure for us, like weight, is difficult to track, as it's not used to pay bills or calculate profit and loss, so it's not already present in most accounting systems. To determine weight requires extra work to find the number of cases bought, which *is* often captured in purchasing systems, and convert cases to pounds. While counting dollars is easier, it puts your commitment's success at risk when prices shift dramatically, as they did when pandemic-related shortages made chicken prices skyrocket above beef's. That caused trouble for those companies who, in order to meet their net zero emission commitments, had moved from actually higher-carbon beef to lower-carbon chicken, but who were measuring their progress by economic value versus weight—and therefore were incentivized to make the higher-carbon choice when costs rose.

Once you've decided *what* precisely you want to measure, the question is, *Can* you measure it? Does your company have an existing system that tracks the attribute you are trying to measure?

To meet Bon Appétit's diversity, equity, and inclusion commitments, we needed to track spend with Black, Indigenous, and People of Color (BIPOC)–owned businesses, but there was nowhere in our accounting system to tag BIPOC vendors and then pull the corresponding reports. That meant keeping a manual list of BIPOC-owned businesses we bought from and manually running spend reports for each vendor every time we wanted a report. It was possible but totally impractical. Being unable to report on a commitment easily, in addition to being poor form, means the goal will be at risk of being forgotten or pushed behind other aims that have easier accountability trails. (We eventually fixed this reporting issue, and it's much easier to track now.) (Shawna Sadowski, who has served in sustainability roles at Clif Bar & Company, Annie's Homegrown, and InterIKEA Group, talks about the critical numbers in our interview on page 140.)

This problem of what to measure when calculating carbon emissions exists across industries. A recent BCG study of nine major industries worldwide concluded that "despite good intentions, companies say they are struggling to cut their emissions in line with targets. Their inability to measure appropriately is the leading roadblock," with only 9 percent of respondents claiming they are able to measure their emissions comprehensively.[10]

Whether you're counting chickens, are a financial services company, or producing glass bottles, you should pin down what and how you're going to measure your progress toward your goals early in your sustainability planning. Think about how you're going to measure the goal when you set it and build the measurement capabilities into your implementation strategy from the outset, not as an afterthought when you're trying to publish an annual sustainability report or an advocacy group comes knocking, trying to hold you accountable.

Measurement Expectations: Wiggle Room

It's tempting to measure against absolutes like "all products will do X" or "100 percent of suppliers will be Y." I advise against it because perfection is impossible. There will always—and yes, I'm using an absolute here intentionally because, in this case, I am confident that 100 percent of companies will encounter this problem—there will always be a reason you don't hit 100 percent.

Someone somewhere will mess up. Either they won't be properly trained, or they'll make an honest mistake. In my industry, this might be an employee not knowing to look for the letters "EFI" in the description of strawberries on the produce order guide and instead opting for the less expensive but not certified berries. Now our promise that "all strawberries are certified to ensure better treatment of farmworkers" is no longer true. Or a supply chain interruption, like a hurricane in Florida, will destroy the entire tomato crop just after you promised to buy only tomatoes from growers participating in the Coalition of Immokalee Workers' Fair Food Program—all of which are based in Florida. Or it could be someone deciding they know better than you, like our client who overrode our commitment to buy pork raised without the use of gestation crates in favor of a brand that inhumanely crated their sows, because at the lower cost, he could cut the meat thicker and he liked thick-cut bacon. Or another legitimate need may override the importance of your policy, like the requirement to serve halal-certified meat to meet the religious requirements of Muslim customers—even though there isn't a rancher that is both following Islamic law and limiting antibiotics use in accordance with your policy.

If you're setting a goal you aim to attain, as opposed to the big hairy audacious variety, give yourself just a little bit of wiggle room on the promise you're making, especially if it's a goal you plan to communicate to customers or advocates.

Step Five: Align All Your Systems to Support Success

OK. You've got your purpose. You've defined terms. You know how you're going to measure. Now comes the time to make sure your administrative systems support your goal rather than hinder it. This unsexy advice may sound familiar—we talked about something similar when defining your mission—but too often it falls through the cracks. When it does, so will your goal. I promise you, even though this isn't a fun section in which you learn about cutting spinach or juicy melons, the material here is some of the most critical. But because it's not exciting, it's rarely tackled as comprehensively as I will cover it here.

Armed with the Farm to Fork program, which we had designed to benefit the farmers as much as our own company, we tried to reestablish a connection to the local food scene by asking chefs like Kimberly Triplett to go to farmers' markets, find people like Brett Grohsgal who were growing biodiverse crops, and bring their products into our cafés. Naively, I thought the farmers would be thrilled to see us. We'd be the corporate white knight riding in to save the small farmer in distress.

Instead, what we heard again and again was, "I used to sell my produce to X supermarket or to Y restaurant, and then I got burned. Supermarkets told me I needed to scale up, and I can't scale up. I don't have any more land. They said I needed to deliver more often. I don't have a dedicated truck driver. They said I needed to meet these expensive requirements, and I can't afford the fees or the time involved. I don't want to deal with corporations and their bureaucracies anymore."

Basically, they were all telling us, "You don't deserve my melons."

We had to prove we were different from other corporate buyers. We had to prove that we wanted to ensure this partner's success as well as our own. We built this trust by creating systems that were appropriate for a small producer and worked for their business by thinking through whether our program requirements made it easier or harder to work with us. Would selling to Bon Appétit truly help farmers' businesses, or will we be putting an undue burden on them with paperwork and added costs that outweigh the potential revenue Bon Appétit will provide? Administrative processes can be counter to your goal.

We set up vendor registration, insurance, and payment terms specifically for small farmers and ranchers in hopes of making it easier to work with us. Most large companies have a purchasing department, or even work with a group purchasing organization (GPO), with the primary goal of cutting costs by streamlining purchasing. That often means consolidating spending into as few suppliers as possible in order to negotiate the best price using promises of a large volume. Purchasing gatekeepers are barriers to local farmers trying to connect with a company. Navigating their systems is a byzantine process, perhaps even intentionally, to reduce the use of nonpreferred or noncontracted suppliers. Local purchasing from dozens of (or in our case more than 1,400) vendors is counter to this sourcing "best practice." Many companies' systems are not only not optimized for working with many small vendors, but are set up to *prevent it* from happening. This is true across industries, whether we're talking food or computer parts.

At Bon Appétit, we did work with a GPO, but we established a "carve out" for Farm to Fork vendors with a separate vendor onboarding process. They had their own special online portal to sign up to be vendors, with simple instructions and streamlined paperwork. It was linked right from our corporate website, making it easy to find. Furthermore, we created a position called a "forager," a point person whose job was to help local producers navigate the systems. We put foragers in every region. We wanted local farmers to sign up, and we didn't want it to be a huge hassle, so we held their hands through the process.

Again, ask yourself: Are my requirements helping us meet our goal or stopping us from achieving it? One of the common barriers to working with any large company is the cost of meeting insurance requirements. Of course, you need to protect your customers and your business, so insurance is necessary. However, have you set limits based on the risks posed by a national supplier and are you now imposing those same requirements on smaller suppliers who present more limited risk? For Bon Appétit, a foodborne illness outbreak caused by a producer that is supplying the whole East Coast is going to cost much more than one linked to a local vendor limited to a few restaurants. (As a veteran of this industry, I tremble even putting these possibilities in writing and have to add *Kaynahora*, as my grandmother would've said, using the Yiddish word to ward off the evil of such thoughts.) Bon Appétit suppliers were required to carry $5 million in general liability insurance, but enrolled Farm to Fork vendors had that reduced to $1 million. If they didn't already carry that level of insurance, we suggested they build in the additional cost to their product price to us to cover the added financial burden.

In food, having a recall plan in place is also necessary, but small producers who sell direct to consumers at farmers' markets don't usually have one. We worked with food-safety experts to create a template for a recall plan that was scaled to the risk of a local supplier, one whose product is sold within a small radius and doesn't change hands multiple times. We then gave it to our Farm to Fork vendors as a starting point for their own plan.

Another barrier for small businesses working with most big corporations is payment terms. For most large companies, the standard payment terms for noncontracted suppliers are 180 days. That equates to "Brett, give me your melons now, and I'll pay you in six months." A small business won't survive paying all its expenses today and getting its revenue six months later. A policy like that is not ensuring the success of the farmer, our true goal. At Bon Appétit, we changed payment terms for Farm to Fork vendors to thirty days and, in some cases, as low as seven.

I've witnessed in our industry and others how these unsexy issues are not only barriers to success with sustainability but also excuses for why they couldn't possibly execute meaningful change like buying from small vendors or local producers. They may still try to market their commitment to local, for example, by relying on large-scale producers who happen to be close by. They can call it "buying local," but they're simply supporting the status quo.

And that excuse-making is not limited to local buying. Instead of trying to support small farmers, you may be consciously trying to find a Black-owned auto parts manufacturer, a LGBTQ+ pattern-making shop, or a temporary labor provider helmed by a woman. Will your administrative systems engender trust in them? Think about where you publish requests for proposals and the jargon you use that might make it hard for a non-native English speaker to complete a bid for your business, how suppliers are onboarded and what documentation you ask for, and every other step in the process of being your supplier.

Brett didn't initially trust us with his melons because he'd been burned by the purchasing practices of big companies in the past. Can you be like Kimberly and actively woo nontraditional suppliers? Meet the business owner at their own operation where they're comfortable and then walk them through your operation to show how their products will be valued. They'll decide you deserve their melons.

When setting your goals, dream. Then root yourself firmly in reality and make sure all your systems are leading toward your aspiration. You don't want your grand plans brought down by an overlooked peccadillo of your accounting system. It's paying attention to these prosaic little details that will enable your success and lead to meaningful change.

Leap Before You Look: Sometimes You Put the Turtle Before the Straw

If you let me, I'll wax poetic on nailing down your systems and insurance and purchasing and policies all day, but to be a leader in the marketplace, you often have to move quickly and set a goal before having all the information on how you're going to achieve it. That means publicly promising something without having any systems in place, or even understanding what they'll look like. Depending on your risk tolerance, this may or may not be comfortable for you. You might have to be a measurement philosophy number two kind of organization to take this on.

Fedele and I work well together in part because he is the big dreamer and wants to set a big goal and go fast, and I am more of the realist, slowing him down with practicalities. As the adage goes, every Kirk needs his Spock, and I play that logical role for my captain. It would be wise in your organization to pair dreamers with realists in a similar way.

Here's how it plays out with us. In 2018, a video of a sea turtle with a plastic straw stuck up its nostril went viral. The vision of this beautiful creature in pain as a marine conservationist tried to pull trash out of its nose was capturing people's attention. Single-use plastics and their environmental impact became public enemy number one.

Fedele was motivated to take action. "We should get rid of straws," he declared. "We don't use that many anyway."

Our purchasing data showed that in 2017, we'd bought almost 17 million plastic straws! I told Fedele we had a lot on our plates already and this was not the easy win he imagined it to be. Trusting my judgment, he dropped the subject for the moment.

About a month later, views of the turtle video were still climbing (eventually passing 100 million views). Fedele raised the idea of paper straws, and with a little quick research, I told him that would mean more than doubling our cost and reminded him we were talking about almost 17 million straws. Not a small expense.

All was again quiet on the straw front until Bonnie Azab Powell, our director of communications, got a Google alert. The UK division of one of our competitors was pledging to stop using plastic straws by 2020.

It was like a gut punch. Fedele had wanted to act. He'd wanted to do the right thing for the environment and be the first to do it. I'd stopped him because I was busy, and it was expensive.

I knew it was on me to break the news and admit I had given bad counsel. But just as I was about to call Fedele, my boyfriend called, so I immediately gave him an earful about straws. "I blew it! No one ever beats us on a sustainability commitment! We're always first!" I railed.

"What do you mean by 'first'?" he asked. Exasperated, I replied, "First to make a companywide commitment, first to implement . . ." A light bulb went off.

We could still be first. The other company's promise had been for a small region. We could go companywide. They were going to make the change in two years. We could make it faster. I could listen to my boss, reduce plastic waste, and maintain our competitive edge, but I needed to move quickly, even if I didn't have a complete plan in place.

I confessed my screwup to Fedele and suggested we now do what he'd wanted to do months ago. He agreed, and I sprang into action. Bonnie started drafting a press release, I reached out to my contacts at Greenpeace who were working on a plastics campaign to ask for a supporting quote, and our national marketing manager started developing print collateral to explain the change to guests. Unfortunately, it was the Friday before Memorial Day weekend, so a lot of people were already out of the office, and we couldn't get precise information. We knew theoretically that paper straws existed, but not where they were in distribution, cost, or availability. That's a lot of unknowns on which to launch a major initiative.

Still, I wasn't going to make Fedele wait again. We decided to move forward without a solid plan for implementation. Bon Appétit would be the first company to commit to eliminating plastic straws, and we'd do it by the end of 2019, a full year before our competitor.

Fedele got excited. I had a groundbreaking announcement. I had a competitive edge. What I didn't have was a clear path to success. I knew it was going to be expensive to substitute paper straws for plastic ones, but I figured that we could mitigate the cost increase by eliminating the use of straws altogether in most cases.

I did build two safety valves into the announcement (wiggle room). First off, even though my hope was to eliminate as many straws as possible, I knew some people with disabilities required straws. We noted that we would keep paper straws on hand for those who needed them. Second, I put the implementation date at the end of the calendar year, which for Bon Appétit meant it spanned two fiscal years. That gave our teams enough time to budget for the price increase in the next fiscal year budget.

That announcement garnered huge attention. There were stories in Bloomberg, national public radio, NBC News, *National Geographic*, Yahoo Finance, *USA Today, Fast Company*—my phone was buzzing with writers looking for quotes. It started an avalanche of other companies taking on the issue and making commitments, which was great. That's exactly what you want: to be the example that triggers others to follow and amplifies the impact.

Everything was going my way. Except, it turns out, that paper straws were a scarce product. So now, thanks to the avalanche we started, the few paper straws that did exist were in great demand and became even more expensive. It was a great time to be a paper-straw company. I tried to coin the phrase "peak straw," using it in several interviews, to say that yes, the price differential was very high right now, but that with all these companies wanting to buy paper straws, hopefully more suppliers would enter the paper-straw market and the price would eventually come down. Simple supply and demand, I hoped.

I also heard from disability advocates. As it turns out, many of the people who need straws because of bite-related issues can't just use paper straws. They need plastic straws because they need a firmer straw that bounces back; a paper straw collapses if you bite too hard. We couldn't eliminate plastic straws completely. That meant keeping them available for all cafés and instructing our people to buy a few for people with disabilities, which would be very difficult to monitor.

And don't even ask me how to drink boba tea or a thick milkshake with a paper straw. As a nondrinker of either, I hadn't considered those needs when I announced the intention to ban the plastic variety.

I had jumped to a policy announcement before having a contract in place to stabilize pricing and ensure availability, before I truly understood the needs of all customers, and before I had an internal system to ensure compliance. Implementation was bumpy, as the availability of paper straws fluctuated. It took the whole year of our phase-in period for the supply to even out. In the end, no one came knocking to ask if we'd eliminated all plastic straws. The fact that in our cafés, straws were few and far between, and the majority of those that were available were paper, was meaningful enough to our customers. Our big hairy audacious move had inspired change in the marketplace, and we'd gotten credit—great credit—so we considered it a success.

Creating brand differentiation through this type of leadership means, by definition, you're going to be doing things that no one has done before. You're working without a map. Blazing a trail sounds cool, and it is, but it also means hitting all the potholes first. My team has heard me say again and again as we bump around trying to find the path forward, "This is what leadership looks like. If it were easy, someone else would've already done it."

What to Do When Initiatives Collide

Occasionally, you've followed these five steps for making meaningful change I've outlined, you're all set up for success, and you're about to make an impact, when you realize some of your efforts are at cross-purposes.

For example, the Better Chicken Commitment I talked about in lesson one, put together by Compassion in World Farming and signed by over two hundred food companies, includes moving to slower-growing breeds of chickens to support the birds' leg health. Conventionally grown broiler chickens take about forty-eight days to grow to market weight.[11] A slower-growing breed might take eighty-one days or more before it's ready to be harvested.[12] Building up muscle mass more slowly allows for the chicken's bone structure to mature and better hold its weight; however, a bird that lives longer also uses more feed, fuel, water, and land per pound of meat, resulting in higher environmental impacts.

What's more important: The welfare of the animal or the toll on our planet? Both are important aims and, in this case, mutually exclusive. Clearly Compassion in World Farming thinks the birds' health is paramount, and it suggests that poultry companies simply raise fewer chickens to offset the environmental impact. Which means that selling more McChickens won't be McDonald's path toward meeting its 2050 commitment to achieving net zero emissions.[13]

I've found myself in other binds like this. I've wanted to support local ranchers but also decrease the amount of beef we serve. I've wanted to serve only seafood rated as Best Choice by the Monterey Bay Aquarium's Seafood Watch program, but I learned several of those "sustainable" species were only available from faraway countries and as fresh, not frozen, meaning they would have to be flown to the United States. That would violate our Low Carbon Lifestyle policy not to use air freight (transporting food by plane can be upward of ten times more carbon intensive than using cargo ships or other slower modes of transport).

Other industries face this too. Electric cars reduce emissions, but batteries create new toxic waste, for example. When facing this type of conundrum, you'll need to weigh several factors:

- *Does one issue speak to the true heart of your brand?* If soil health is fundamental to your brand, as it is for Stonyfield Organic

yogurt, that may mean buying organic sugar from Brazil even
though, for many other reasons, such as supporting regional
food systems and reducing transportation impacts, you'd rather
source it closer to home in Louisiana or Florida.[14] Similarly, if
you're a vegan clothing brand, you may choose to use polyure-
thane for your "leather" jackets because, even though plastic
is less environmentally friendly, reducing animal cruelty is the
very heart of your brand.

- *Is there an external group applying pressure?* In the case of the
  Better Chicken Commitment, Compassion in World Farming has
  been joined by most leading animal-protection groups, including the Humane League, the Humane Society of the United
  States, Mercy for Animals, and others. This is a powerful bloc.
  Refusing their ask will surely result in public action. To that
  same point, you should consider the reaction of labor unions
  whenever you're contemplating a process or policy change if
  your workers are under a collective bargaining agreement. Does
  the more sustainable option create more work in some way for
  your employees? If so, are they going to be compensated? Unions
  are masters at getting press and applying public pressure.

- *Is there a higher authority?* When sourcing halal-certified meats,
  there is literally a higher authority: Islamic law. Suggesting customers bypass their personal religious beliefs for the sake of a
  public health issue such as antibiotics overuse is something I
  wouldn't do. By the way, halal practices also prohibit stunning a
  nonviolent animal before slaughter, but controlled atmosphere
  stunning (CAS) is required for the Better Chicken Commitment.
  The groups behind the Better Chicken Commitment have yet
  to address this conflict. Sometimes that higher authority is
  labor law. A tech company wanting to differentiate itself based
  on embracing work/life balance could have a conflict between
  offering employees more control over their schedules and state
  overtime regulations.

- *Can you simply avoid the issue?* Chefs might want to serve fresh Aquaculture Stewardship Council–certified salmon flown from Norway, but they don't have to. Wild Alaskan salmon can be bought frozen at sea, which if handled well is even better quality than fresh. Rather than trying to monitor worker safety at a factory in Bangladesh, can you move your manufacturing to a country with relatively stricter labor laws such as Costa Rica or the Dominican Republic?

I've asked myself each of these questions when weighing colliding initiatives. I signed on to the Better Chicken Commitment and looked for other ways to reduce our carbon emissions to account for the increased impacts of the chickens living longer, told our chefs to get creative with the long list of species that are both Seafood Watch–approved and not air-freighted, engaged in groups supporting regenerative agriculture research in hopes of getting our local cattle ranchers on pasture credit for sequestering carbon, and offered halal meats with a sign informing guests that they don't meet our antibiotics policy.

When initiatives collide, ask yourself how the issue fits within your brand's ethos, if external pressures exist, and what the cultural nuances are; decide if the issue needs to be addressed; and make compromises but explain why to your consumer.

Now That's What I Call Meaningful Change

A year after Kimberly Triplett started buying melons from Brett Grohsgal, I got a call from him asking if he could feature us in an article he was writing for a publication called *Growing for Market*. He wanted other farmers to know how great it was to sell to an institution and how they could supplement their farmers' market business with a strong relationship with a food-service company.

I knew then that the Farm to Fork program was going to work, and we would have a positive impact on flavor and the businesses of small farmers. We were doing more than checking boxes. We deserved Brett's melons!

Bon Appétit's Farm to Fork program eventually grew to include over 1,400 small farmers and food producers and over $40 million spent annually on flavorful food. That money supports the local communities and helps farmers stay on their land. That's meaningful change.

ACTION ITEMS

How to Make Meaningful Change

To successfully build a brand on sustainability, you must go beyond what's already easy to do in the marketplace and take an action that creates a meaningful change to a supply chain or common practice. You have to act first, focus on a specific outcome, and work tirelessly to create a positive impact on your community or the environment.

These five steps will ensure you're making a real change in the world, not just positioning your company as following a trend:

Step one: Find your purpose. Clearly define why you're setting a sustainability goal and what you're trying to achieve.

Step two: Find a leverage point. Identify the action you can take that will catalyze change in the market. Find your power but be careful how you wield it.

Step three: Define your terms and parameters. Carefully define the language used in your commitments and establish guardrails that will help you achieve the spirit of your goal rather than merely reach a numeric target.

Step four: Set your targets and measure. Decide if you are going to set a reasonable goal that you know you can hit or a BHAG (big hairy audacious goal) that may inspire you to go further but you'll ultimately fall short of achieving. Then pin down exactly how you're going to measure progress and build a tracking mechanism. Word to the wise: don't write absolutes like "100 percent" or "all" into your target. Leave yourself a margin for error. You'll need it, trust me.

Step five: Align all your systems to support success. Make sure your company's policies and administrative processes all support achieving your goal, rather than working counter to it.

Making Change Meaningful

WALTER ROBB
Former co-CEO, Whole Foods Market

I once ran into Walter Robb in the corridor of San Francisco's Davies Symphony Hall. He looked like a little kid about to see a rock-and-roll god. He was indeed there to watch a hero perform, but it wasn't Mick Jagger. It was author, activist, and farmer Wendell Berry, interviewed live on stage during the 2008 Slow Food Nation festival. During the "show," I watched Walter scribble furiously in a notebook, trying to capture everything the agrarian philosopher said.

Walter has spent his career proving that retail—like eating—is an agricultural act (to riff on one of Berry's most famous lines). Needing to fuel performance as a student athlete at Stanford University, he'd learned the importance of healthy eating and stumbled into opening a natural food store in 1977. He eventually went to work for his friend John Mackey, running Whole Foods' twelfth store.

The sense of mission, to sell food that was better for the customers and the planet, was palpable and drew Walter in with the opportunity to do something that felt meaningful to him. He eventually rose to co-CEO, overseeing more than five hundred stores, and has been credited with helping make organic food mainstream and redefining what we expect from the grocery aisle.

When it comes to sustainability, how do you differentiate checking off a box versus making a meaningful change?

In my experience as a leader, when you stand up, the number one thing that people are looking for is, are you giving them the straight shot? Are you being truthful? That's the number one thing they're thinking, whether you're talking about job layoffs or about a sustainability program going forward.

Meaningful change is created with an honest beginning, a worthy goal, and then clear steps to hold the organization accountable and follow through on what's been said. Absent that, it can easily just become another thing that falls by the wayside or gets put up on the shelf or doesn't get taken seriously. We've had a few of those over the years, and some that were sincere but just didn't work.

It starts with thinking it through thoroughly from the standpoint of all the different stakeholders, how they're going to respond, and what information they're going to need. There needs to be a real commitment from leadership of "This is what we're going to do, this is the hill we're going to take." Done that way, it becomes a source of pride for the team to realize that their company is going to be the one to do that. Then it's really embraced by the team members, and that becomes the foundation for meaningful change.

I'm ready for the T-shirt that says, "Change starts with an honest beginning and a worthy goal!" Can you give an example of how you implemented that philosophy?

With respect to the animal welfare standards, the big shift—the meaningful change—was to take into account how the animals were treated in addition to the economics of selling the meat. The obstacle we ran into was that the industry wasn't really set up to make animal welfare part of their go-to-market. So, we set up a series of meetings with all the stakeholders, including the nonprofits, the science-oriented organizations, and the producers. Where we had the leverage was that we simply said, "Look, we're going to have a robust discussion and try to reach a consensus, but if we don't, we're going to make the final decision because we're the ones selling [the meat]. You're going to participate in creating these standards, but in the end, there's going to be a time when you have to make the changes, and if you don't make the changes, then you're not going to be able to be a producer for Whole Foods anymore."

It was a combination of both the carrot and the stick, right? The carrot was, "Help us do this and come along and make yourself a better organization." The stick was, "If you don't, then you're not going to be able to sell to Whole Foods."

It was a meaningful change because it represented a significant and permanent raising of the bar for the production of animals. We had to overcome the inertia, the comments that this can't be done, doesn't matter, or is too expensive, all the objections that you could expect from folks. We worked through those by having a fundamental insight that raising animals according to their natural behaviors was the right thing to do for Whole Foods and to set the standard in the marketplace. That whole process was run by Chatham House rules [anyone who participates is free to use information from the discussion but is not allowed to reveal who made any specific comment], so nothing could be ascribed back to individual growers who were complaining. We had a series of meetings that included people who had been enemies in the marketplace—whether it was the anti-animal-agriculture organizations, the vegetarian organizations, the scientists. The attempt was to basically facilitate dialogue with all those groups to come up with something that people could live by. That process went on for a few years. The [Global Animal Partnership] five-step standards [for animal welfare] came out of that.

I will say that I think it was slow to get embraced by the customers because they already expected that from the meat that Whole Foods sold. The team members appreciated it right away, but meaningful change sometimes takes a little while to land. We thought, "Wow, we did all this work. We met with all these people. We went through it all. And then the customers didn't really understand it." So, you have to stay with it until they do, and you have to double down on your education efforts. It took a couple of years for it to really gain traction with the customers. And that change was real.

A few years of development and then a couple of years until appreciation are a lot. Would you describe yourself as patient?

No, I wouldn't. I'm almost seventy now. But no, I was a real pusher. I felt like my job was to push the organization and to push these changes, so I was pretty high energy in terms of movement. I would describe myself as intense, passionate, and competitive.

How have you made purchasing decisions that stood the test of time: differentiating your brand in the marketplace, making meaningful change, and factoring in bottom-line costs?

To quote our grocery bag, Whole Foods has been pioneering food standards since 1980. Really the difference, the core of Whole Foods, has been the food standards. What's in the food and what's not in the food. Whole Foods started with no artificial anything in the food and grew from there to setting very specific standards by category of product.

An example of a meaningful change that we adopted even though it seemed counter to good business on the face of it was the Monterey Bay Aquarium's Seafood Watch standard. We all understand that 71 percent of the planet is covered with oceans, and the oceans become sinkholes for the carbon that's released. Also, a number of species were threatened because they were not being caught sustainably. Our position, after doing the work, was to stop selling the red-listed fish [the species categorized as "Avoid" by Seafood Watch], which was sort of counterintuitive for a retail organization—to walk away from sales. The fact that the change seemed to have potential for an adverse economic impact adds to our credibility, though. People think you're being serious about the issue if it looks like you're walking away from sales. In the end, you walk forward, because you get a better reputation as an organization that has integrity.

On the day that we announced that decision, I personally got a lot of emails and texts from team members about how they were pleased and proud of the organization for taking that step and walking away from sales. They saw us as leaders in the marketplace, and they themselves therefore were part of that pride of being leaders. This was an example of a company living its values and putting those values into action. Meaningful change can make a meaningful difference in the culture.

Was it always clear which change to make?

We had a disagreement within the executive team as to what step to take with GMOs. At the time, GMOs were a raging debate. Genetic modification is really only in eight crops, and nonmodified corn and soy are basically goners in the United States in terms of the penetration [of GMO varieties], but it was a big debate. The five of us had a hard time coming to a conclusion about it.

On the one end was, "Look, they're already out there. The organic standard says no GMOs [so those who want to can avoid them]. They're part of the world, and there's nothing wrong with GMOs. We should just move forward." Then there were those who felt like we shouldn't carry them at all. Then there's the middle ground of "What does the customer want? The customer wants the right to choose. So, let's label it so they can make the choice."

Another point is that we didn't want to get locked into something and have science unfold some new information. That's something that I learned from John [Mackey], to think through where this decision is going to take us five or ten years from now.

That was one of the most heated conversations among the executive team. Meanwhile, our customer group was saying, "Somebody say what we should think about this," because it was such a big issue at the time, with Monsanto pushing Roundup and GMOs and the USDA not really saying anything. People were looking at Whole Foods as a leader that hadn't taken a position on this issue, in a marketplace that really wanted somebody to step up and lead. The team members were also getting antsy because we had not taken a position on something they felt was really an issue of the day.

We finally concluded that we were going to label things so that people could make their own decision. What struck me was that it took us a long time, and we fell behind in terms of the team members' expectations of the company. The learning was that sometimes the pressure for change comes from within an organization. The ones who had the leverage were the team members saying, "What are we doing on this?" We were slow to respond and come up with an action step. They pushed us.

Was there a time when what felt like the meaningful change didn't equate to what advocates were asking for?

When we created Whole Trade, we were in dialogue with Fair Trade, but their rules were limited only to co-ops, and we wanted to have our program, our dollars, go to for-profit enterprises as well as nonprofits. [Fair Trade USA does now certify large for-profit companies based on their labor standards, but that change was made after the introduction of Whole Trade.] The desire was to create our own brand that we could own and bring to our customers throughout our range of products. It was an effort to provide some sense of responsibility for purchases made outside the United States, because Whole Foods buys products from well over eighty countries.

The Whole Trade program was really just about calling out products that were bought in the developing world and that met certain standards for quality. Whole Trade's shelf life ended and was changed to Source for Good, because Whole Trade didn't really take into account the social side. It didn't try to measure how team members on the farms were treated or how they were paid, any of those sorts of things, as criteria. Sometimes you have a solution to a problem and then it evolves, and you've got to sit down and work it through and figure it out.

Did customers ever ask for a change that felt counter to what Whole Foods should do as a business?

People asked us to create a farmers' market for produce in our parking lots. From a standard standpoint, the answer would be no, because it would take away produce sales, but from the win-win relationship-building scenario, our suppliers liked it, our customers liked it, and the communities liked it. When you looked at it from the multiple-stakeholder angle, we did in fact try, and sales went down in the produce department, but the goodwill that was generated with the communities and with the farmers was the return that we got. So sometimes what looks like conflicts can actually be win-win scenarios. You just have to think more creatively about them.

Since leaving Whole Foods Market, you spend your time as an adviser, mentor, and investor to the next generation of food businesses. What advice do you give founders?

The number one thing I always ask companies is, What is your purpose for being? What is your mission and what are your values around that and how do you go to market? What is your customer saying they like and don't like, and so therefore, what changes do you need to make, whether it's a name change, a product change, or a change to your process?

The word that comes to me is *leadership*. Abraham Lincoln famously said there's two types of leadership. One is where you tell your constituents what you are going to do, and the other is where your constituents tell you what they want you to do. Both are appropriate forms of leadership. There are times when your customers are helping you see what you need to do. And then there are times when you're deciding, you're going to take a step forward in service of your values, and you're going to show your customers exactly which way the direction should go.

When I work with companies, I try to encourage them to really build a lane that reflects who they are and what they're trying to do. The younger generations are looking to align with products that resonate with their own beliefs. And so, how are you addressing the concerns they have about the environment, with respect to social conditions, with respect to product quality? How are you addressing those desires of the customers in products and services that you're offering? Understand who your customer is and how you can serve them, and what changes you can make and still stay within the boundaries or integrity of your values.

Interview

How to Stick to Big Hairy Audacious Goals

LISA DYSON
CEO and cofounder, Air Protein

With the rise of Impossible Foods, Eat Just, Perfect Day, and about eight hundred other alternative protein companies that have garnered over $11 billion in capital investment, you could call the quest for a sustainable animal substitute a modern-day gold rush.[1] That makes Lisa Dyson, who is creating protein out of thin air, the alchemist of our time.

Lisa was inspired by NASA research done in the 1960s to explore the possibility of producing food for extended missions to Mars by combining microbes with the carbon dioxide exhaled by the astronauts. NASA never figured it out, but Lisa is using her PhD from the Massachusetts Institute of Technology—where she became the fourth Black woman to earn a doctorate in theoretical high-energy, nuclear, or quantum gravity physics—to make this magic vision a reality.

Her product combines microbe cultures, CO_2, nitrogen, and oxygen in large fermentation tanks to create usable protein within hours. Powered by renewable energy with no need for arable land, pesticides, or genetically modified ingredients, and able to be produced anywhere in the world, much less the solar system, Lisa's technology could be worth its proverbial weight in gold. (Full disclosure: I sit on the board of Dyson's company, Air Protein.)

Like the gold rush a century prior, though, some indicators point to a looming bust in the alternative protein market. In 2022, shares of investor darling Beyond Meat fell by 75 percent, and the frothy interest in alternative proteins started to dry up. Many of the herd of startups had to pivot. The questions became what to compromise and how to transform. Founders were ousted, and the industry started to look chaotic.

Lisa, however, remains calm. She has a North Star—a BHAG.

You start every presentation with a set of assertions that define Air Protein as a company. Why are you so diligent about that?

Having started a company before, I know how easy it is to get distracted. There are so many directions you can go. If you have a bunch of innovators [as employees], then they're potentially going to go in many of those directions. That's why focus is so important for a startup. You want your startup to focus *and* to dream big.

Everyone must have the same goal, the same North Star, but there's more than one way to get there, so you empower the team to figure out the path. They may come up with some roads that we've never thought of before, but you need to let them know where we want to end up.

When in the life cycle of the company did you sit down and define those parameters?

Before it started, because of the experience I had at the other company I founded, Kiverdi. I found early on that if I was in a brainstorming session and talked about some things that our technology could potentially do, three weeks later members of the team were trying to prove out those new functions at the expense of the work they were supposed to do. Essentially, the vision—convert CO_2 into the raw materials for everyday products—was too broad. We got off track.

Then I discovered Patrick Lencioni [author and management consultant specializing in executive team development and organizational health] and his six questions. Why do you exist? What do you do? How do you behave? How will we succeed? What's most important now? And who must do what?

I just love this as a framework and used it right at the beginning of Air Protein. We added the BHAG to that as the North Star.

What is your big hairy audacious goal?

To set the context, the food industry produces more greenhouse gases than the entire transportation sector. And it is a key driver of deforestation. Specifically, meat is the biggest offender. So, we as a company exist to accelerate the world's transition to climate- and rainforest-friendly meat. We do this by making nutritious, delicious meat using the most sustainable protein on the planet. All that context leads us to our BHAG, which is to become the number one meat company in the world.

How are you defining the "number one meat company in the world"?

We're not! It's plain and simple. It can be number one in many different ways. Number one by volume, number one by market cap, but some measure of number one. We're so far from that now that it literally doesn't matter. The point is, we shoot for the biggest thing we can do.

Your BHAG doesn't mention sustainability.

That's right. That's where Lencioni's questions come in. What expresses sustainability is "what" we do: we make nutritious delicious meat using the most sustainable protein on the planet. If, for example, we choose to use [more economical but less environmentally friendly] gray hydrogen, we're not making the most sustainable protein on the planet. We've now shifted away from the what. We're now a different company. Our BHAG can't stand alone.

My suggestion to other companies is to bring the whole thing together—the what, the why, and the how, because if you're acting in isolation, you may not achieve what you're really trying to achieve. Our "why" is to accelerate the world's transition to climate- and rainforest-friendly meat. That means that our what has to help us do that. Then our BHAG doesn't need to be encumbered by a whole bunch of extra words. It's just "to be the number one meat company" because we've already defined everything else separately.

If Air Protein becomes, say, a $10 billion meat company and displaces millions of pounds of animal-based protein, you won't be the number one meat company in the world, but will you still be successful?

The short answer is absolutely, but it's not over. We'd still be growing, right? We will be on a path of success. We will not have met that BHAG until we are actually the number one meat company in the world, but the success is in the journey, and if we get to $10 billion, I would be thrilled.

How do you keep the team focused on the North Star?

At least once or twice a quarter, we go through that framework with the entire team. New people are joining, so we review the basics. Also, the answers have been tweaked over time. It hasn't been static. For example, we didn't include "rainforest-friendly" in the beginning, but then we realized that that's important, too. There's a bigger environmental story that we're addressing. Our why expanded, which may impact decisions we make later.

So, every quarter, once the leadership team has revisited and set the answers in stone, we bring it to the broader team. It's important because people may discover something. "Oh, this protein could be used as a fertilizer!" They can get caught up in some other innovation, and you say, "Oh, no, no, come back to what we're doing. We could do lots of things, but let's do this thing. Let's make nutritious and delicious meat using the most sustainable protein on the planet."

The road is not straight, so we make sure the road has three-month stop signs, and we pause and reconsider. We may need to turn right a little bit; we shift our direction, but we always have our eyes on the prize because of that North Star. If you don't verbalize it, some people might think we're making protein bars or something else, and that's a whole different set of work. Instead, let's verbalize it, let's all focus on the same goal, and then empower the team to figure out how we get there.

I'm surprised to hear that what seems like fundamentals of the company, the BHAG, and what you do, could change as frequently as quarterly.

The market dynamics change, and your company is not going to survive if you aren't agile and can't pivot. Let's say the price of what you were making just dropped by two-thirds; then you step back and quickly reassess what you're doing and your technology, your innovation, and then answer the questions again. Revisit every single one of those answers and the questions every single quarter and don't get committed to what you said in the last quarter. If the context has changed, then you may need to change with it. No matter if you're in a big company, small company, startup, whatever, you have to be able to change direction or you'll follow your star right off a cliff.

Embed Goals; Set Targets

SHAUNA SADOWSKI
Sustainability development manager, InterIKEA Group

Shauna Sadowski grew up on a family farm in Saskatchewan, Canada, so she knows the difference between the idealized image of agrarian life and the reality of it. She's also got academic cred, attending the University of Pennsylvania's Wharton School of Business for undergrad and later earning a graduate degree in agriculture, food, and environment from the Friedman School of Nutrition Science and Policy at Tufts University, where Kathleen Merrigan, future US deputy secretary of agriculture, was her adviser.

She parlayed both her upbringing and her education into a sustainability career with stops at Clif Bar & Company, Annie's Homegrown, and General Mills. And today, working at IKEA, she's expanded her view beyond agriculture to include forestry, and beyond the US consumer to include customers in fifty countries. She's scaled up her perspective but hasn't strayed far from her core belief that a connection to the farmer and to the land, as she witnessed in her youth, is critical to our future.

When you left the farm to go to Wharton, did you imagine that there'd be an agricultural component to your career?

Not at all. I grew up on a farm where making a living was hard. I was very much that kid who said, "I don't want anything to do with the farms." Everyone around me told me I'd have no money—nothing. That was kind of the mentality I came from. I'm one of seven kids, and we all up and left.

But after I finished undergrad, I went into management consulting, a typical path out of Wharton. I knew inside my heart that I needed something that was going to tie back to people, the human side of things. Then I read Eric Schlosser's seminal book, *Fast Food Nation*. American food and politics were becoming a part of popular culture and that showed me that the link was food.

I remember seeing a documentary, *Troublesome Creek*, about a farmer losing his land, not making enough money, and his stuff getting auctioned off. I left bawling. I hadn't made the connection of the hardship I faced as a kid and the impact it had on what I was doing, but I'd never really moved myself so far from it. I'd thought, "That's behind me," but no, it *is* me.

It was only at that point that I even realized agriculture *was* food, and all that means. Even though I'd grown up surrounded by it, I'd never connected the two.

My career since then has been corporate sustainability, but it's always come back to asking, "Who are the people that are at the ground level, and what's really happening on the land?" knowing that the farmers can contribute to the positive change we seek.

Taking on sustainability is daunting. Where should a company start?

What is your business fundamentally doing? Focus your efforts there, and other things should become less important. Understand the context of what you do as a business. For food companies, it's about agriculture, right?

In CPG (consumer packaged goods), it was packaging, packaging, packaging! But the more you look into the science, you know it's about your ingredients, your business model, what you source.

Food packaging is not irrelevant, but it's not as important as the ingredients.

Having both traditional business training and a focus on intangibles like connecting to the land, how do you think about setting targets?

"The numbers" are what everyone else in business relates to. In sustainability, you need a baseline to create a meaningful target. If you don't have a solid baseline, you've got to be creative in the way you set targets. Use what you have.

For example, soil health was a key outcome we wanted to have an impact on at Annie's, but how do you measure that as a buyer of food, not a grower? We were using organic as a proxy. That's how we started to develop a way of quantifying things, recognizing we didn't have the exact information we needed, but we did have proxies to stand in as we continued to develop an understanding of what was happening on the ground.

As we dug in, we learned that in some cases organic was better and, well . . . in some cases, worse. Oftentimes it was based on the practices used and the regions in which they were based. That's what led us down the path to regenerative agriculture, which was all about how we understand the practices that farmers employ and the differences those make.

Do we even know enough to quantify that? This gets back to your question, how do you set targets? Well, you have to understand the context first. Maybe your target becomes just to get more information. It's fuzzy and amorphous, but that's actually what's needed most versus "reducing by 20 percent."

That's not the precision that you expect to see or how financial decisions are made. For someone who's a sustainability practitioner, that becomes our bigger challenge.

Did goals like "gather more information" or "soil health" meet the needs of the organization?

I tried to make those sorts of goals relevant through our annual sustainability reporting. I also partnered with marketing to figure out clever ways to share the information with consumers. The real intention of those goals, though, was to drive our internal decision-making, to make sure we were working toward the outcomes we were seeking. I was at companies trying to do things differently.

The needs changed over time. Annie's became part of General Mills, which created a separate group called the Natural and Organic Operating Unit, encompassing several brands including Annie's, Muir Glen, and Cascadian Farms. At that point, we tried to embed our goals into the P&L because that's how public companies understand performance.

We were trying to create a more holistic idea of performance, including environmental and social outcomes. We renamed our department the Triple Bottom Line Unit. We knew our financial metrics and our marketing metrics, and we wanted to put environmental and social metrics side by side with them.

The numbers are the way we have been trained in business, yet they only tell part of the story. That's part of our jobs in sustainability: to still embrace that, but also broaden it. It's about systems thinking. Targets out of context are just numbers that don't mean anything.

Science is always revered: "Listen to the science!" Well, you can have bad science, too. You can have science that's just reductionist and doesn't account for the total system. Everything is part of a system. It's how the science is done—the methodology itself—that matters. The results are determined by the methods; therefore, understanding the methods will help one understand if the results are worthy.

How did you elevate sustainability to be on par with financial performance?

Right before I left General Mills, we were working on embedding sustainability goals into the quarterly reporting the company made to the investment community. The goal was to report on the different environmental KPIs alongside the financial ones, so sustainability wasn't always seen as separate from the P&L. Sustainability reports are always looking backward, but quarterly reporting includes projections. We were trying to insert sustainability targets that were forward-looking, that we should be driving toward, as part of corporate governance.

That makes the stakes for sustainability pretty high. Did you ever miss a target?

Yeah. I mean, YEAH!

It's funny because you can set targets as high or as low as you want. In the area of sustainability, we're trying to do things on a high-impact, high-deliverable scale, but it's complicated, and there were plenty of times we didn't succeed. Then the question was, how do we share that? What do we share about it? Who gets this information?

Context becomes even more important. At Annie's, we looked at the percentage of our products that were organic, and we were trying to have that number go up, because we wanted to have our brand be more and more representative of organic agriculture. It didn't always go that way. Sometimes, the percentage actually went down, so we'd have to say, "How do we think about this and how do we put this in context?"

We would try to evaluate it on multiple scales. For a product to have the USDA Organic seal on the front of the box, to be "certified organic," it must be made with 95 percent or more organic ingredients, but you can market a product as "made with organic" if it has 70 percent or more organic ingredients. So, the number of certified organic products was going down, but the overall percentage of organic purchases was going up because we had more and more made with organic products.

Different ways of looking at the data told different stories. Net net, we were doing the right thing, even if it looked like we were missing a target.

Is it possible to solve a complex problem with a packaged food?

A proof point that that's possible and an internal reason to celebrate came from the pivotal work that we did at Annie's to bring the regenerative agriculture story to store shelves.

When I first started at Annie's, I was keen to bring farmers more into the conversation, but I didn't have a procurement person at the time who understood that or could see how it could happen, so it wasn't a focus. Over the years—actually after the General Mills acquisition—I formed a partnership with marketing and found a willing person in purchasing. That was the trifecta! A relationship between sustainability, marketing, and sourcing allowed this beautiful product to come to store shelves: a regenerative-ag mac and cheese!

The sourcing person found the farmer, my team substantiated the science, and the marketing person brought the story to life and made sure it all penciled out financially. That was one of the proud achievement moments!

The package had graphics of soil on the front with little pictures of mycorrhizal fungi so you could see from the shelf that soil matters. We talked about carbon sequestration. We talked about organic. It was a great example of how you do something authentically and meaningfully.

We set up a huge display at Expo West [the premier natural products trade show] that brought these issues to life, brought biodiversity to life; we brought farmers, and we talked about soil infiltration and the importance of soil health and soil organic matter with retailers. All the geeky stuff that we love! We made it into something that others who maybe aren't as connected could appreciate as well.

The product eventually had a limited run at a handful of stores. Consumers might not have been quite ready for it, but it started conversations.

Even though the product didn't catch on, you still consider regenerative-ag mac and cheese a win?

Oh, absolutely. Even just getting the senior management team at General Mills to support it was huge! And eighty thousand people come through the Expo West trade floor. That big stage amplified and elevated the story. You could hear the buzz.

We also learned so much. One of my biggest lessons was from the marketing people who showed me the importance of telling the *why* behind it. I was really focused on the what and the how. I always thought of the why as inherent, but it wasn't.

A lot of time was spent getting that message right. We created this big, beautiful, internal storyboard and kept asking ourselves, "Why does regenerative agriculture matter?" and "Why does agriculture matter to a food company?" and making sure our campaign gave the answers. We said, "Look, these events are happening—the fires in California, the droughts devastating agriculture. And guess what? Soil is part of the solution! And, food is about agriculture!" That awakening I'd had so many years earlier, right?

That was a good win!

Lesson Four

How to Fix It When
You Fall Short

"Hey yo, what up. This is Evan. I work at Belcampo Meat in Santa Monica. I just want to let you know, everyone know, this company claims to be selling meat straight from their farm. That's not true. They're fucking lying to you."[1]

So starts a video posted to Instagram by Evan Reiner, who shows photographic evidence of beef and poultry from a variety of producers in the Belcampo walk-in refrigerator—even though the high-end meat purveyor claimed to raise all their meat on their own farm.

Then he shows USDA Choice–stamped beef on the cutting board of the shop that boasted only organic and grass-fed beef product. "Their shit's not local. It's from Tasmania," says Evan as he holds up a tender-loin sealed in a package from Cape Grim Beef prominently citing their roots in Australia. "Don't let these people lie to you like this."

Reaching more than thirty thousand views, his May 2021 video made the *Los Angeles Times*, Eater and other food industry news sites, and even international outlets such as the *Guardian*.

A few days later, Belcampo cofounder Anya Fernald took to Instagram herself to "deeply apologize for the mislabeling and poor sourcing in [Belcampo's] Santa Monica location." She "emphasize[d] that what happened in that shop doesn't touch our mail order or grocery products," just those sold in Belcampo's own retail shop, but she acknowledged that "it's a meaningful issue regardless of its size. It could be one steak and it's hugely problematic."

Not everyone accepted Anya's apology. In June, Justine Freedman filed a class action lawsuit against Belcampo on behalf of any customers who "unwittingly" paid higher prices for "falsely advertised" meat from the company.

In October, five months after the video, Belcampo CEO Gerry Embleton issued a statement to Eater LA confirming the closure of Belcampo's retail business: "While we are ending e-commerce, retail, and restaurant operations, the company is exploring a range of options to provide consumers with non-branded products through new distribution channels. The company's supply chain, farm, and processing facility are [all] best in class, and we hope that there are opportunities to collaborate with companies eager to provide consumers with meat products that meet those high standards."[2]

In December, the *San Francisco Chronicle* published a damning article about Belcampo's growing troubles, including a federal investigation of its processing plant for "an array of sanitation, safety and labeling violations."[3] The USDA inspectors' reports also cited "improperly labeled meat months before the scandal broke, which contradict Belcampo's claims that the mislabeling was isolated to a single butcher shop in Santa Monica" and the CEO's assertion that the processing plant was "best in class."

Today, the Belcampo farm is a "glamping" site, replete with canvas tents and fairy lights, listed for rent on Hipcamp.com. The website for the meat company seems to no longer exist.

It's an astonishing cautionary tale playing out over a breakneck seven months that should serve to warn anyone who wants to promote sustainability but doesn't pay attention to the details. Greenwashing, or intentionally misleading the public to appear more environmentally friendly, can be the death knell of a brand selling sustainability. From loss of face to loss of an entire business, the consequences are swift and serious. It didn't have to be this way. If Belcampo had followed their own slogan, "Meat you can trust—transparency from start to finish," they might still be a viable brand today.

Glossing over what might seem like boring details is tempting, especially for a broad-speaking inspirational CEO, but that nitty-gritty level of understanding operations and how a commitment is playing out in the business is exactly what leaders need to focus on, to keep your promises and to keep your disaffected employees from slamming you on Instagram. Remember how I played the Spock role fixated on the reality of implementing our sustainability initiatives, allowing Fedele to be a big-picture-focused Captain Kirk? Perhaps Anya Fernald was missing a first officer who kept an eye on the reality of Belcampo operations.

It seems obvious to say the antidote to greenwashing is transparency, but I don't think most companies understand or have the stomach for the *degree* of transparency they must achieve. They want to choose what to show and what to leave a little opaque. Sustainability can only be achieved through a radical openness that will make many of you uncomfortable. To be fully transparent, you must adopt several tenets for how you operate:

- Don't overpromise

- Be clear and truthful about your journey and how it's going

- Own your failures—be first to tell people, in your own words, when you fall short

The Belcampo story, for example, wasn't black-and-white. The company did invest heavily in creating a more sustainable business, and they got things right much more often than they got them wrong. But when their model started to crack, lack of attention to key details and a miscalculation in the response strategy was the difference between the survival of a trusted brand and the obliteration of a company in mere months. As your path to creating a more sustainable business is sure to include major potholes, learn from the Belcampo case. These steps will help you avoid tripping.

Step One: Get into the Weeds

Belcampo did eventually admit they had misrepresented more than a single steak. Once they got into the thick of it, their internal investigation calculated that "externally sourced meats which did not meet Belcampo quality standards represented 6% of the total value of all meats procured from the beginning of 2020 to the end of May 2021."[4]

Six percent!? Another way of looking at that number is that they got it right 94 percent of the time. That's actually pretty good.

I'm not being sarcastic. Here's why. Supply chains are complex, ever-changing, and hard to keep perfect, especially when your product is derived from a living being, not a factory-made widget. A disease outbreak causes animals to reach market weight more slowly than anticipated, equipment in the slaughterhouse malfunctions, truck drivers go on strike—when you're running a business with one farm, one slaughter facility, and very few options for pivoting, like Belcampo, you're going to have product shortages. Their sin wasn't being short of product 6 percent of the time; it was pretending otherwise.

Had they simply placed a sign in their meat case saying, "Due to extreme weather conditions surrounding our farm in Gazelle, today we're offering Mary's Free Range, Organic Chicken from Pitman Family Farms," there would have been no drama. Yes, putting up that sign would clutter the beautifully designed butcher case and muddy the pristine image of Belcampo, but it could also have saved the company. It would have served as a signal. For, if every time there was a product substitution made, someone at the corporate office had to create a sign and disseminate it to all the impacted channels, there probably would've been a lot more executive focus on shortages, and Anya wouldn't have found the video "heartbreaking" because she would've been well aware of every substitution. The company's reaction to downplay the incident as isolated likely was as much because the leaders weren't in the weeds, understanding the shortages and how they manifested in their fragile supply chain, as it was an attempt at spin.

During the Covid-19 outbreak in 2021, we at Bon Appétit—much like Belcampo and countless other companies selling meat—weren't always able to offer products that met our own standards. We made a lot of signs. And, when we tallied our end-of-year report on compliance with our purchasing policies, the numbers were significantly lower than previous years. Let me tell you, I would've been thrilled with Belcampo's 94 percent compliance rate.

Supply chain problems notwithstanding, we were transparent about our shortcomings, and not a single customer or client complained. This is the only way for a sustainability-focused company to avoid greenwashing: you must overexplain your systems and challenges so that *you* tell your story, not Evan on Instagram. (Evan was terminated from Belcampo. Worried that other butcher shops were loath to hire him because of his history as a whistleblower, he tried to get an all-beef hot dog business called Droogies Ultra Dogs off the ground with a big emphasis on, as he says, "doing things right."[5])

I've seen the Belcampo mistake many times, in many industries. The cliché that the cover-up is worse than the crime rings true here. No matter your business, owning up to your shortcomings will always be less painful, and less damaging, than trying to pretend they aren't there or fibbing about them.

Step Two: Sweat the Details

With your sustainability program, be clear when you're being aspirational. Use phrases like "Our goal is . . . ," "We strive for . . . ," or "Our policy is . . . ," rather than making definitive claims such as "All of our . . ." or "100 percent of . . . ."

At Bon Appétit, we used to advertise that "our ground beef is Certified Humane and raised without any antibiotics ever," but in practicality, that wasn't true 100 percent of the time. Sometimes an ill-trained chef would order the wrong product, a few small cafés were in remote areas where we didn't have enough buying power to bring our compliant beef into distribution, or the supplier would run out of our beef and make a substitution. In other, rarer cases, we had major supply chain disruptions such as during Covid-19. I changed the statement to "Our contracted ground beef is Certified Humane and raised without any antibiotics ever." Adding the key word "contracted" indicates we have an agreement with a beef processor to supply our cafés with ground beef that meets a set of specifications, which include an 80/20 ratio of lean beef to fat, no neck meat, never given antibiotics, and certified by Humane Farm Animal Care. That doesn't mean that 100 percent of the ground beef we serve meets those specifications at any given time. Had we continued to promise that 100 percent of our ground beef was Certified Humane, we would have made ourselves vulnerable to a "gotcha" moment. Instead, we try to tell our story with honesty and attention to detail. Even during historically catastrophic challenges to our supply chain, we have maintained our integrity through accurate messaging.

Words are important, but this lesson also rings true for the visual representations of your company. Painting a too-pretty picture of sustainability is an all-too-common pitfall of marketing teams. One of the most basic—while often unintentional—forms of greenwashing is using images that misrepresent your supply chain. Make sure that whoever is picking the photos for your posters, packaging, and website understands how the product you sell is produced. When touting that your chicken is raised without antibiotics, an unwitting graphic designer might use a beautiful image of a red hen scampering around a pastoral farm. However, most broilers—as chickens raised for meat are called—spend their whole lives in barns packed in with up to forty thousand other chickens. No antibiotics, maybe, but also no grass, no sunshine, no quaint chicken house.

I don't expect anyone to put a photo showing the reality of a dark barn dense with chickens in their marketing materials. I certainly didn't. What I did do, though, was always use close-up pictures of chickens that didn't give context for where they were. And I made sure the chicken was white, because every industrially raised broiler I've ever seen was white. On the other hand, cage-free layers, which are also raised in barns, tend to be breeds that have red feathers. Ask your supplier for important details before starting the marketing design process otherwise you end up depicting something other than reality.

Step Three: Don't Promise Perfection

Dan Barber is the executive chef and co-owner of the Michelin-starred restaurant Blue Hill at Stone Barns in Pocantico Hills, New York, that has long been promoted as a model for restaurants' power to transform the food system. Their stated mission is "to create a consciousness about the effect of everyday food choices." Dan himself is viewed as a front-runner in sustainability-focused fine dining. But he learned the hard way the pitfalls of overpromising perfection.

There's no question Dan is committed to building a more sustainable food system. Yes, he's had an unusually sweet situation in which to do that, given his restaurant sits on an idyllic eighty-acre nonprofit farm and education center on what used to be a Rockefeller family estate. But he's not just walking foodies through fields of grazing sheep to their tables in a vine-adorned barn so they can snap pics of his tasting menu and make their friends jealous on social media. He focuses his efforts on the nitty-gritty, too.

He's drawn needed attention to some unsexy but important topics. His TED Talk on the nuances of farming fish, aka aquaculture—not exactly Kardashian-like clickbait—got over 2.5 million views.[6] He wrote *The Third Plate: Field Notes on the Future of Food*, a 483-page vision for a food future that goes beyond the usual emphasis on eating seasonally to discuss the natural rhythms of livestock and explain why eating whole grains and small portions of free-range meat can contribute to personal and planetary health. It was a *New York Times* bestseller. Heck, inspired by Dan's seed startup, Row 7, we got several farmers to plant new varietals of vegetables.

He's made meaningful change. And yet the influential food website Eater dedicated over 3,500 words to debunking many of Dan's claims about *how* meaningful—basically accusing him of greenwashing. It wasn't that Eater was denying that his ideas about sustainable food were good ones. It was that Dan presented to the world a perfect version of those ideas and appeared to claim that his restaurant embodied that utopia.

One of the allegations in the Eater article, which highlighted many of the embellishments (to put it kindly) Blue Hill at Stone Barns used to promote itself, is that their famed "Badger Flame beet tartare" sometimes contained other local beets in addition to the specific Row 7 Badger Flame beet that Dan helped design. A medley of local beets?! *Quelle horreur!* This isn't exactly the same as Belcampo substituting commodity beef for its supposedly pasture-raised, free-range steaks. Do people really care this much about *beets*? It doesn't seem like that would be a major issue—except that Dan and Blue Hill had presented the dish as using only the Badger Flame beet, because that would be the perfect manifestation of Dan's vision. And when you present perfection, people delight in finding and sharing the flaws.

In a long, written response to the story's author, Blue Hill representatives admitted "there were occasions—especially between 2014 and 2019, when there were limited supplies of the beet—when we used local yellow beets as a puree to complete versions of a Blue Hill dish called Badger Flame beet tartare. But the Badger Flame beet always constituted the bulk of the tartare and defined its flavor (which is what we were noting in particular). Given these two facts, we did not call attention to the other beet contributor as it simply operated to support the Badger Flame beet."[7]

If Dan really wanted Blue Hill to be a "a model that can be replicated anywhere," it would've been more helpful for aspiring chefs to know the details, like the secret trick of combining different varietals of beets.[8] As one sous chef told Eater, "When you're saying things are possible when they're not possible, it's an unattainable goal no restaurant can achieve."

L'affaire beet was part of a pattern of embellishing stories told tableside or to reporters, in which the detail that Blue Hill was supplementing dishes with ingredients was left unmentioned. Eater wrote: "Blue Hill explains this practice as one born out of the unpredictable nature of farming seasons—an example of the way that the restaurant told stories about seasonality and small-scale farming while often opting to shield guests from its limitations and disappointments."[9]

Blue Hill and Dan Barber fell short in a completely avoidable way, one that we also saw with Belcampo. I find many companies are victims of their own desire to appear to the world to be as far along the road to sustainability as possible. Their desire to simplify the message and win hearts and minds leaves them exposed to damning accusations when people find out the facts of what's happening. Instead of using his own restaurant as an example of the complexities and nuances of trying to change the food system and being honest about those challenges with his customers, Dan presented perfection. And perfection is hard to live up to. Blue Hill should have been telling the world about the challenges of cooking this way and how to overcome them. If a poor growing year yielded a less-flavorful crop of Honeypatch Squash, simply add a drop of butter rather than abandon the experimental veggie that Row 7 Seeds touts developing as "longer-storing," "single-serving," and "packed with beta carotene," all important attributes when trying to create a more sustainable food source.[10] Teach people to meet the challenges of a nonuniform, sometimes unpredictable food system (or whatever complex system your company is part of—maybe it's shipping, or telecommunications, or building bikes—it doesn't matter; all businesses have these kinds of challenges) so they will be more willing to accept the limitations and work with them. Pretend it's easy, and they'll feel like failures, give up when they don't get the same gorgeous dish you showed on TV, and then be really pissed when they find out you pulled the cruelty-free wool over their eyes.

The truly frustrating part of what happened to Blue Hill at Stone Barns and Belcampo is that often the exposé of imperfections leads people to overcorrect and think, "Well, that business has *nothing* to teach us about sustainability because they were cheating." In fact, Blue Hill and Dan have incredibly good ideas. Admitting it's a challenge to get them to work gives texture and will draw interest to your story in a way that pretending to be perfect can't. Everyone loves to hear about struggle, setbacks, and the triumphant power of butter!

Be it a beautiful presentation of the bounty of local beets or an impressive record of 94 percent of meat raised on your own farm, your story is always better in your own words, warts and all. Perfection is not as impressive as precision. You're more believable when you admit challenges.

How to Get It Right: Admit When You Fail, and Fix It

"I've got more money than I can spend in a lifetime, and for some reason I care about these pigs, so I guess I'll spend my money on this," explained activist investor Carl Icahn to a *Wall Street Journal* reporter asking why he was waging a proxy battle against the board of the McDonald's Corporation.

Behind on their commitment to "eliminate the use of gestation crates" in their US pork supply chain—note the perfectionist, absolutist framing—McDonald's tried to quietly change their promise and the lower-bar goal to source pork from "sows not housed in gestation crates during pregnancy." Unfortunately for McDonald's, the staff of the Humane Society of the United States noticed, as did Carl.

Here's a quick refresh on the issue of gestation crates, which I mentioned in lesson one: these are crates not much bigger than the breeding sows themselves and in which they are placed for the entirety of their four-month pregnancy. They can't move or turn around in these crates. They have observable animal welfare side effects. Renowned animal behaviorist Dr. Temple Grandin compares the practice to making a human live their life in an airline seat.

The billionaire founder of Icahn Enterprises, known as one of the foremost corporate raiders, had initially become interested in animal welfare when his daughter, Michelle, worked at the Humane Society a decade earlier, around the time McDonald's made their original gestation-crate commitment. And the financier put his mouth and his money behind the pigs, funding two new candidates for the company's board of directors: president of Green Century Capital Leslie Samuelrich, and me.

When someone as high profile as Carl Icahn takes a stand, people listen. Stories appeared in the *Financial Times*, Bloomberg, the *Economist*, the *New York Times*, on CNBC, and were syndicated to outlets around the country. More than twenty institutional investment houses holding McDonald's shares set up meetings in which Carl, Leslie, and I pitched our plan for better corporate governance at McDonald's. The burger behemoth hired their own crisis management team and spent roughly $16 million to counter our candidacies.[11]

To say McDonald's bungled its pork policy is an understatement. The sin wasn't falling short of the original commitment, though. It was trying to pretend the company hadn't stumbled, then failing to put a plan in place to eventually meet the original promise to treat animals in a way that millions of people, including Carl Icahn and me, think is more humane. Instead of trying to find a messaging loophole for their continued use of an outdated production method—the writing is on the wall for gestation crates, as they've been banned in six countries and nine US states—McDonald's should've followed NYU professor, podcast host, and popular pundit Scott Galloway's three pillars of crisis management:[12]

1. Acknowledge the issue

2. Top leader takes responsibility

3. Overcorrect

I know firsthand how to use this three-pronged approach, based on a similar switcheroo I had experienced with a supplier years earlier, when our pork supplier, Smithfield Foods—the very same one that McDonald's uses—had asked that we quietly change the language of our policy from "gestation-crate-free" to "group-housed." I had just checked into a Hampton Inn en route to some meeting somewhere when I was tipped off to this simple-sounding but suspicious change of wording. I was tired and wanted to crawl into one of the side-by-side queen beds with my notes for my meeting the next day and some microwaved popcorn. But this couldn't wait.

I reached out to Smithfield Foods' executive vice president and chief sustainability officer, with whom I'd been having discussions for four years about improving welfare practices, ever since he'd come to see us in Palo Alto. I thought I'd been very clear about our desire at Bon Appétit to eliminate the use of gestation crates. Eliminate, not reduce, was what I'd said in our multipronged animal welfare commitment made three years earlier—a commitment that was coming due in eight months. As I understood it, Smithfield was doing just that, and I'd promoted the change very publicly—in our marketing materials; on a panel at the Chefs Collaborative annual conference, sitting alongside pork experts Paul Willis of Niman Ranch and Barry Estabrook, the James Beard Award–winning author of *Pig Tales*, a book about the pork industry that covered small farms to pork factories; and for thousands of attendees and online viewers at TEDx Manhattan.

To his credit, Smithfield's vice president responded straightforwardly. He said the phrase "gestation-crate-free" was not 100 percent accurate, because all producers use gestation stalls for the first five or six weeks after artificial insemination until they confirm pregnancy. He sent me a company-produced YouTube video describing Smithfield Foods' timing from crate to group housing.

My blood boiled as I watched an actor explain the benefits of putting a pregnant pig "in her own individual private stall" where she stays for "five or six weeks" and gets "lots of food," with graphics of ice cream and pickles as if she were a happy mom enjoying some pri-

vate time to get her funny cravings satisfied.[13] Recasting the inability
to turn around or walk as getting "plenty of rest" was, in my opinion,
deceiving at best and deceitful at worst. The illustration of the pig was
even wearing a hair bow and earrings! These cartoon sows were not an
accurate representation of the reality of life in a gestation crate, and
the length of time in group housing was not what I'd meant when I'd
said "gestation-crate-free."

Even though it was late, I called Josh Balk, who you may recall was
my contact at the Humane Society of the United States who'd sent me
the videotape that led to our cage-free-egg policy. By then Josh was
senior food policy director at the Humane Society. I ratted out myself
(and Smithfield). I acknowledged the issue. If we weren't living up to
our commitments, he was going to hear it from me first.

Next came a rather heated meeting with representatives from
Smithfield on neutral ground, a windowless conference room in an
office park in North Carolina. (People who dream of jobs making food
systems change may picture walking through bucolic fields, but much
of the real work is done in generic meeting rooms or behind a computer looking at a spreadsheet full of pivot tables.) An animal scientist
representing Smithfield warned me against anthropomorphizing the
sows (wait, who made that video of pigs with hair bows? I wondered)
and said the gestation crates were better for the pigs, providing them
safety from their aggressive peers. I countered that there were other
ways to lower aggression, like managing the temperature of the barn
and giving these highly intelligent animals things to do other than
harass each other.

We went back and forth—my voice getting louder, them calmly
repeating their party line. Finally, exasperated, I said, "We're never
going to agree. You're going to keep pulling out studies that I'm going
to say were funded by industry, while you're going to say I'm just listening to the animal welfare activists. Let's go to the one person we all
know has only the pigs' interest at heart: Temple Grandin."

Temple Grandin is a professor of animal sciences at Colorado State
University and a consultant to agriculture operations of all sizes in the

design of slaughterhouses and other facilities. She gained some fame first from *Thinking Pictures*, a book she wrote about how her autism allows her to see things as an animal might, and then a lot more fame in 2010 when a movie of the same name came out starring Claire Danes. She remains a respected expert by both sides of the animal welfare aisle, industry professionals and advocacy groups alike.

"If Temple Grandin says you're right, I'll continue to buy pork from Smithfield," I stated. "If she says the gestation crates aren't needed, either you pull them out or we pull our business from you. And I'll tell this story and name names." Oh, they were going to see some acknowledgment of the problem all right!

As we'd hoped, Temple gave a very balanced opinion, noting the progress Smithfield had made in reducing the time in gestation crates and encouraging the industry to strive for seven to ten days in crates, just until insemination, not until the confirmation of pregnancy. She also touted "exit stalls," an alternative to gestation crates that allows sows to enter and leave the crates freely, as a better solution.

As promised, I took Temple's word and said I'd agree to the shorter time in crates and the use of exit stalls. Smithfield, instead of complying, said goodbye to the Bon Appétit business, suggesting we find a different supplier.

So I did. Our purchasing team called on every big pork supplier we knew. They were all using gestation crates until the confirmation of pregnancy or even for the whole gestation period. We contacted all our Farm to Fork pork farmers and asked if they could scale up. "Yes," was the answer, followed by the big "but"—"by a few animals at most." Nowhere near enough to satisfy our guests' desire for bacon or ham. We found premium producer Niman Ranch didn't use the crates at all, but the economics of a program with them were impossible.

Finally, Josh from the Humane Society bailed me out. Rather than chastising Bon Appétit for our inaccurate claims, Josh teamed up with us to solve the problem. He recommended the Clemens Food Group, a large, privately owned Pennsylvania pork company that we had never heard of and that, for their Farm Promise brand, had gotten their gestation-crate use down to just three to ten days. I contacted Clemens, explained what I'd heard and what I was looking for, and asked if I could tour the facilities that supplied the Farm Promise line. They said sure, without hesitation, which was a great sign.

A few weeks later, I was suited up in my brand-new pair of granny-style undies seeing those facilities with my own eyes. My host Bob Ruth, then president of Clemens Food Group production division, showed me the few rows of gestation crates that remained in each massive barn. The sows in crates immediately conjured the image of a prisoner in solitary confinement. The animals had no way of interacting with other beings, and to say they were confined was an understatement. The metal surround only allowed room to stand or sit. The sows were practically immobilized. Add to that the density of equipment, which made the room dark, creating an even more dungeonlike feeling. It was like these pigs were being punished.

In another part of the building, large open pens housed a few dozen sows together. Several cuddled up against one another, another played with a large metal chain, and a few warmed themselves in the sunlight streaming through the windows. Bob jumped over the railings into the group pens and, at his invitation, I did too. We walked among these giant creatures as they nuzzled our hands and clothes.

"This is one way we can tell whether our workers are doing a good job," he said. "The animals should feel relaxed around people." And indeed, they seemed to. I noted that everyone I met on two full days of farm visits treated the sows and their piglets warmly and affectionately.

I also learned to my great excitement that the pigs used in their Farm Promise brand were never given antibiotics or ractopamine (a popular growth promoter that other countries have banned), which meant that this pork would fulfill another one of our goals: to move away from animals routinely given antibiotics for growth promotion or to treat illnesses caused by their living conditions. Ractopamine wasn't yet on our animal welfare no-no list, but we were happy to be able to say our pork producer didn't use it.

All of this better pork came at a price premium, to be sure, but I decided the issue was important enough to justify this price increase. Just in time for our end-of-2015 deadline, we signed a contract with Clemens and began the process of getting their products into our distribution system. And I reluctantly rewrote our website and marketing materials to say, "Our pork comes from sows raised in group housing" rather than "gestation-crate-free," because even Clemens's industry-leading minimum time in crates wasn't the same as "free."

I wasn't done yet. Overcorrection was still needed. I put out a press release scoring Bon Appétit's compliance with our own various animal welfare policies. There were some successes, but mostly things we still had to do. We shared that we had made great progress but were transparent about our failures: our pork wasn't gestation-crate-free (we explained why); due to avian influenza, we were six months behind on switching to cage-free liquid eggs, and the more expensive Clemens Farm Promise pork had made it harder to meet our promise of 25 percent of meat, poultry, and egg purchases coming from producers with third-party-certified animal welfare practices.

Despite our shortcomings, Josh and the Humane Society praised our progress in the press release. He understood why we'd fallen short where we had, and yet he was still willing to applaud our efforts because we'd gone further than any other food-service company.

The lesson I learned from all this: make a true attempt to do the right thing, be open about your failings, and you'll be applauded as a leader.

Then I invited Barry Estabrook, the author I'd spent a lot of time with at conferences, to accompany me on a visit to Clemens and write about their approach to group housing. Clemens agreed, including allowing a photographer to document their facilities. In a country where the meat industry has managed to get six states to pass so-called ag-gag laws making it illegal to unofficially visit, photograph, or videotape industrial farms—and more would like to ban visitors entirely—that openness once again set Clemens apart.

Barry published a fair, and fairly positive, piece in *Modern Farmer* magazine, and I told the story in my own words on the Bon Appétit blog. I didn't name names though, until now. I can only imagine the look on the faces of executives at Smithfield when Carl Icahn proposed me, of all people, for the board of McDonald's, a company buying a volume of pork that Smithfield could not easily walk away from. She's baa-ack! It might have been years later, but I knew they would had not have forgotten me.

In the end, we lost the vote for the board seats, but changes were afoot for McDonald's—and for pigs. McDonald's shook up their corporate office, announcing the departures of the chief financial officer, global chief supply chain officer, and chief global impact officer.[14] The phone of the Humane Society's Farm Animal Protection team started ringing: other companies with similar gestation-crate commitments coming due wanted help implementing their own policies to avoid such a public battle. It seems McDonald's, and the newly unemployed members of their executive team, had learned the painful consequences of greenwashing.

By the way, it took me an additional seven years, but I eventually moved Bon Appétit's pork purchases to a line with zero days in gestation crates. Clemens Food Group, with input from Temple Grandin, figured out how to do it in 2021, and Bon Appétit was the first company to roll out the product nationally. Overcorrection complete!

ACTION ITEMS

How to Fix It When You Fall Short

Creating a brand based on sustainability requires a radical, even uncomfortable, openness, especially when you fall short of your goals.

Follow these four steps to avoid the common pitfalls of greenwashing.

Step one: Get into the weeds. Overexplain your systems, challenges, and any deviations from your company's standards.

Step two: Sweat the details. Be clear when you're being aspirational and use phrases like, "We strive for . . ." and "Our goal is . . ."

Step three: Don't promise perfection. Share your *whole* story, warts and all. Perfection is not as impressive as precision.

Step four: Admit when you fail and fix it. Acknowledge the issue, take responsibility, and go above and beyond to correct it.

Interview

Activists as Allies

JOSH BALK

Cofounder and CEO, the Accountability Board; cofounder, Eat Just

It's appropriate that the book that shaped Josh Balk's approach to corporate advocacy, Dale Carnegie's iconic *How to Win Friends and Influence People*, starts off with advice about food production: "If you want to gather honey, don't kick over the beehive." A dedicated vegan and animal activist, it's not in Josh's nature to stomp on habitats, so as Carnegie suggests, he begins relationships with warmth and compliments instead of the scare tactics some of his advocacy brethren employ.

It's worked. He's gotten many of the largest food companies in the world to improve animal welfare in their supply chains, while also establishing real friendships rather than making enemies. But Josh saw another route to motivating corporations to make change: shareholder action. He was inspired by activist investor campaigns, such as the one I participated in to get McDonald's Corporation to end the use of gestation crates. He formed the Accountability Board, a new type of advocacy organization that has bought shares in almost every major publicly traded food company and "tracks companies' environmental, social and governance (ESG) performance, actively engaging to increase transparency and progress."[1] He's at least giving the beehive a good shake.

How do you decide when to be positive with corporate engagements and when to become the enforcer?

I want to start out relationships, whether it's with people or companies, thinking the best of them and let them prove otherwise. If you can start in the positive frame of mind, you can build what I would hope is the best type of partnership there is, a collaborative friendship working together to solve issues. I continue that for as long as they keep proving they are that way.

Companies show true intent on addressing an issue when they take tangible steps. And when I say "tangible," that doesn't mean they reach the end goal overnight. I mean when they say, "Hey, Josh, here's the plan we came up with; we're going to do a certain percent year by year to get to the end goal. I know, Josh, you wish we could get there overnight. But this is the plan we came up with." If the plan is even a too-long phaseout of some practice, I still appreciate that there's a plan. It shows that there's some thought behind it and some actions being put in place to actually move forward. Then I know that the company is sincere in their endeavor.

When we started, we were thrilled and giving applause when a lot of the fast-food chains and consumer packaged food companies were switching 2 percent of their eggs to cage-free. That was a step forward. What we applauded was that they did something; they went from zero to 2 percent, while simultaneously saying that they were committed to fully resolving the issue. That action, meager as it may seem, demonstrated that the company was willing to address it.

But not every company is going to be that way, right?

I start getting a little concerned when I don't see any action, getting no response to my inquiries. When we have meetings, there's no update whatsoever, but a lot of corporate-speak. Folks may think that we're naive and don't understand, but when there's a lot of jargon and fluff, all we hear is "nothing, nothing, nothing, nothing, nothing."

I don't know why companies do it. In reality, all companies have to do to show sincerity is get started. If companies just did that, they would be in a dramatically better position. And this goes for making the world better—and for me, so much of my life is trying to make the world better for animals—but even if I didn't have any ethics whatsoever, and I was the CEO of the company, I would do it because frankly, what I'm asking companies to do, it fits within business models. As a CEO who had no ethics other than profits, I would do things that fit with a societal view and what people expect companies to do.

Just start, take steps, and then keep taking steps and give updates. Companies like Bon Appétit might miss a target; for us, it's "Hey, let's work together and resolve it" versus McDonald's that, when they miss a target, tries to rewrite history and pretend they're on track. I say, "OK, we need to change who is on your board right now."

The difference is that you have demonstrated real significant strides to get to the goal, and you were candid with us directly about the challenges versus never telling us that there were challenges. Then, when pressed by us saying, "Company X, you pledged to be 100 percent gestation-crate-free by this date. Where are you? Why didn't you provide any updates whatsoever?" The Company X reverses, saying, "Oh, we had challenges."

When did you have challenges? When I asked you? Or did you have challenges before but never told anybody about it? How can I trust you now when you weren't transparent about the challenges until you were approached about missing your deadline? Then all of a sudden, these challenges occurred? That's where I start to get real concerned with companies.

Another good litmus test of whether companies care is if they say, "I want to work on this issue of confinement, but I don't know what suppliers can meet it." I'm really in tune with the industry, so

I'll send a list of suppliers like I did with you and Clemens [for the gestation-crate issue]. The company should jump on that. I'll follow up with the supplier and say, "Hey, Clemens, did you hear from Maisie?" If they say, "No," that's a good indication the company isn't sincere.

People are scared to tell you they have challenges, because they think it'll somehow be used against them. Is that a well-founded fear?

When I hear challenges that are specific, that's when I appreciate the relationship with the company more, because I know they've been working on the issue. When I hear broad challenges, I know the company is stalling.

Here's an example. In 2023, *Covid* was the easy word to throw out there. Companies had ten years to phase out caged chickens, and when I call them out in 2023 for not reaching their commitments, they bring up Covid. Really? Covid started in 2020. What did you do for 2015, 2016, 2017, and so on, to address this issue before Covid existed? And the answer is likely nothing.

The more details we hear about the challenges, the more confident we are that the company is actually taking the issue sincerely. And, by the way, when the company proactively tells us their challenges—not after a shareholder resolution is filed, not after we go to the board— no, proactively tells us, that's when you know they're sincere versus making excuses.

For example, General Mills said, "Listen, we are actually ahead of where we're supposed to be on getting rid of gestation crates in pork, but we're behind on eggs because there's been an outbreak of avian influenza." I was not concerned, because they also shared they have a contract with an egg supplier to go cage-free when stocks return. There is a glide path. I said, "Why not put in your sustainability report that you have contracts?" and they said, "That's a great idea. We will put in our ESG report that we have contracts in place to meet the commitment." That's what I see as sincerity.

Can you easily detect greenwashing?

Whenever I hear companies talk about how much the treatment of animals matters to them, without being very specific, I think there might be some greenwashing. Companies who do good for animals are specific about what they're doing. I cannot tell you how many times I have read ESG reports from companies talking about the critical importance of the treatment of animals in their supply chain with so much flowery language related to the issue. And then when you look for details, they're nonexistent.

There's a benefit there, though. I like it because now we can call them out for the things going on in their supply chain that counter the fluff they're putting out. There's a CPG company that said they believe in the Five Freedoms [a decades-old definition of animal welfare set by veterinarians and animal behaviorists] and that's part of the mandate within their supply chain. Well, that company had no policy to get rid of gestation crates or battery cages [what laying hens are confined in]. So literally, it was false.

We filed a shareholder resolution, calling out the company for blanket lying. And we knew they were lying because we told the company ahead of time, "Hey, you can't have these words while simultaneously this is going on." They failed to change their claims. So, it's not like they didn't know and said, "Oh my gosh, someone wrote that? You're right. We've got to change it." We notified them about the hypocrisy, and they just refused to address it, because it looks so good to have those words out there.

So we wrote a resolution and pointed out that, if the company is so willing to blatantly lie about this issue, what other requirements does the company claim to have for suppliers that the suppliers are not following?

Immediately the company reached out saying, "OK, what do you guys want? Let's work together to remove this shareholder resolution." Now that company is moving to become cage-free and get rid of gestation crates. So, I like it when companies do greenwashing. Then we get to call them out on it.

What about the tactic some companies take to stay under the radar? Don't take a stand, don't make a commitment.

They go to the instincts we all have as kids when we close our eyes thinking something's going to go away, or we put our heads under the covers because it's a scary movie. That doesn't leave us, even when we're adults. When a company tries to ignore an issue, especially an issue that is as high profile as animal welfare, it's the kid closing his eyes thinking that that's going to make the issue go away. Once the eyes open, the issue is actually worse.

Say you're a company and you don't want to have a spotlight on you. Be transparent, take steps forward, be proactive in saying, "Here's where we're at. Here's our challenge. Here's some plans to overcome the challenge. What are your thoughts?" And the spotlight goes off. There is no spotlight when things like that happen and tangible progress is occurring.

Instead of trying to pass an ag-gag law, farmers that are doing a good job want people to visit their farms. Some companies try to pass laws that make it a crime for you to visit.

What a board member, vice president, or director at the company should know is that they are doing the company a favor by addressing these issues; they are saving serious headaches to come. Eventually issues like animal welfare boil up to the level of the board of directors, a shareholder resolution, or the SEC or FTC, or the level of reaching out to their sell-side analysts who tell investors to sell. All this pain is something that the company could prevent by working to address the issue. A lot of folks who've dealt with serious shareholder campaigns, if they were being truthful, would say, "Yeah, we should have just done this. It wasn't worth holding on to the old practice."

What do you think a company should do if they are falling short of meeting a commitment?

One, if a company is sincere in their work and really cares and wants to prove that they're sincere, they should proactively reach out to a partner or even the group pressing them on the issue and say, "Hey, I just want to check in with you proactively to say we're running into a problem." That's rare, and they would be lauded by whoever received that email.

Two, have ideas for solutions. It's not just "Boy, we got a problem," but also "We've thought of these ideas to resolve it. They might not be the best ideas, but we're working on it." If they have no ideas, that just tells me that they have no interest in working on the issue. Then I provide ideas, and if they just tell me they won't work without specific reasons or giving alternate ideas, I know they don't care.

Chipotle missed a target related to Certified Humane chickens. I did an interview for Bloomberg, and the reporter seemed a bit hopeful that I would bash Chipotle. But I defended them, saying, "Listen, they acknowledged that they didn't meet the target before they were even approached, and they are committed to meeting it. And by the way, they have a history of doing well, especially compared to competitors." To be clear, that's the type of company that we applaud when they're open about missing goals. In no way do I view being candid about a challenge as something negative from a company that's done well and has a plan to solve it.

Let's talk about this little company that you founded, Eat Just, which has achieved unicorn status, a valuation of over $1 billion. Your motivation for starting a company was to end animal suffering by reducing the need for eggs. But the messaging for the company is all about the environment, not animal welfare. Was that a conscious decision?

My motivation was certainly animals, and early on, to investors, there was a component of the message about animals. There were numerous slides in the pitch deck that described chickens in the egg industry in battery cages and the male chicks being ground up alive. [In the egg-laying industry, male chicks are culled shortly after hatching, some by maceration in high-speed grinders, because they're seen as useless.]

Our first investor was Khosla Ventures. This wasn't some person who cared about animals and gave money during a friends-and-family round. We were talking to one of the largest, most serious venture capital firms in the world, and Vinod Khosla was motivated because of the animal welfare story. He hated the idea of the chicks being ground up alive. So, we used it in pitch decks.

With buyers at food companies, it was different. It makes sense to always be honest while simultaneously focusing on the issues that are the most effective to talk about. At the beginning, we were selling mayonnaise and cookies. I don't think that the retailers or food-service companies that buy those products want to start talking about cruelty to animals in their supply chain, because it doesn't feel good. It is a bummer to talk about animals being tortured. Cruelty to animals is so visceral; it might not be effective in getting buyers to listen. Instead, we said, "We can help provide a product that can fit a lot of needs. Your company already has commitments on climate change, it already wants to provide options that can meet the needs of people with allergy issues, and it already wants to provide more plant-based offerings that are mainstream and not something just sold in a local co-op. This is a type of product that I think will fit for mainstream consumers, it helps people eat a bit better, and it's just as delicious." Making that argument is frankly just more effective.

On the cultivated-meat side, a more recent product [in which meat is grown from cells cultured in a lab], "Other Josh" [Josh Tetrick, Josh Balk's childhood best friend and the cofounder and CEO of Eat Just] has talked about things like "slaughter-free meat." In Singapore, where it's being sold, the government has called it "cultured meat," so he uses that terminology to be respectful, but if one looks at interviews, he always uses slaughter-free meat, which is pretty blunt.

Is that because the target consumer buying Just Chicken would have a different motivation than somebody buying Just Mayo?

People buy mayonnaise because it tastes good on their sandwich. They don't think about the eggs in it. They might not even know it *has* eggs in it. Then we start talking about animal cruelty? They say, "What are you talking about? I just want a spread, and now we're talking about chickens being abused for this?" It gets confusing, and I get that. Whereas it's very easy to picture that meat comes from animals for slaughter. Very few people don't know that part. It's just an easier correlation.

What else did you learn about messaging, from being on the product side instead of the advocacy side?

One thing that Other Josh did very well was keep talking about how we've got to make the right thing the easy thing to do. Most people do not want to cause harm. But we live, and we all cause harm. I do. You do. We all do, in our own way. Who wants to be scolded? So, the argument Josh made early on is that these products allow people to do the right thing because it's easy. And what makes it easy? It tastes mainstream. You'll like it; I'm not asking you to give up taste for some hippie product that tastes terrible, but you're doing it to save planet Earth. You're going to enjoy it.

Also, it's sold in the mainstream places where you already shop, like Walmart, Kroger, and Safeway. You don't need to go to some natural food store that's a hundred miles away to find it. Even the packaging doesn't scream in your face, "Planet Earth!" or look hippie. It's just normal. So, guess what? It's going to taste good, and, by the way, as you enjoy it, the world is a bit better off.

It's a lot more embracing than a bummer of a message: "Did you realize when you don't buy this mayonnaise, you're an animal torturer?" "Do you realize that you might as well just light the planet on fire when you buy that?" Who wants to hear that?

The other thing is to talk ordinary. Sometimes when we work on issues of real concern, we use academic language. We talk like everyone knows the issue as well as we do. That's something Eat Just does as well as anybody. Maybe it's because Other Josh was raised by a single mom and played football, so he always wondered how to talk to the people he grew up with about what he's doing. I was raised by a single dad with my brother, a bunch of sports people in the household. I don't forget where I came from, how to talk with them. Do I talk about "utilitarian calculations regarding suffering of creatures?" I know they will say, "Josh, let's watch the football game."

That's something that companies sometimes forget. When I read ESG reports, it's like the experts in ESG write for other experts, not customers. If they gave the report to a family member who's not involved in the issue, that person would have no idea what the heck they just read. I think that's a problem.

What was Unilever's reasoning behind suing your company over the name "Just Mayo" and how did you respond to the lawsuit?

The first product we offered in grocery stores was Just Mayo. It was mayonnaise made without eggs. It got a lot of media attention. Bill

Gates said that we were one of the top three companies that would forever change the food system. It won the CNBC Disruptor Awards. So, keep in mind that the product was made, and the company was formed, to make the world better. We were all in a meeting at the head-quarters, which was then in a garage in San Francisco, and Josh was served legal papers. We were all completely shocked. Unilever, one of the largest food companies in the world, was suing us! And it was about the mayonnaise because it's called "mayo"! [Unilever alleged the "Just Mayo" name misled consumers into believing the product contained real eggs.]

Fairly quickly, it became a call to action for the company, because it was such an act of bullying. At the time, there were just several dozen people working in that garage, and Unilever was bullying this small group who was trying to make the world better.

My guess is they thought either we would be so scared, we'd do any-thing to resolve it, or we'd spend so much money on legal fees, we'd go out of business. It had the opposite effect. The lawsuit fired us up.

The basic message was "Bring it on!" and instead of cowering in the corner being afraid, guess what, we made media calls to the *New York Times* and *Wall Street Journal*. Unilever, hope you enjoy being made fun of by David Letterman about this. By the way, we're going to let all the NGOs out there that work on the issues that we care about, like climate change, animal cruelty, and issues related to children and allergies, know what Unilever did. And I hope you enjoy what your social media pages look like after that.

This is just speculation. I'm guessing it was likely twenty-four hours later, Unilever realized it had made a mistake. All the news was 100 percent positive for us.

Positives came out of it, then?

Eventually their CEO reached out to Other Josh and said, "We're going to withdraw the suit, and maybe you can fly out here and let's talk, because I think we're probably more aligned on things than we perhaps realized." It was certainly a very exciting moment and turned out to be one of the highlights in the history of the company.

Unilever is actually one of the better companies on the issues that were the driving force in the creation of our company. Ben & Jerry's [owned by Unilever] was one of the first major companies to go cage-free [on eggs], because of a campaign by the Humane Society, which was only about a week long. So, of all companies, the suit by Unilever was surprising.

There are a couple lessons from that case. One is that it is much better for large incumbent companies to embrace innovation than to try to stifle it. They tried to stifle more shifts to plant-based products and just came out looking like a bully. They miscalculated where an ordinary consumer stands when a global conglomerate takes on a startup company that's trying to make the world kinder, solve climate change, provide food that's healthier.

It's a lesson for all big companies. You want to embrace the future. Look at startup companies and say, "Hey, they haven't had the momentum of being a large company. They aren't stuck in a cycle of going around like a hamster on a loop and just thinking, 'Hey, what we're doing is good!' and not having a mindset of 'What could we look at for change that we haven't thought of already?'"

What an amazing story it would've been if Unilever partnered with us rather than trying to stifle the company and getting all this negative backlash. Likely they would have been years ahead of where they ended up when they did launch a plant-based mayonnaise. They would have looked like a real trail trailblazer, rather than the big conglomerate that tries to slow down any positive change in the world.

How to Tell Your Story

For the pilot launch of Bon Appétit's Circle of Responsibility marketing campaign highlighting our sustainability initiatives, I had a big poster-sized board made blaring the headline "Circle of Responsibility" and the program mantra, "At Bon Appétit, we take a macro view of wellness. We believe a healthy environment, community, and menu are all vital to the well-being of our guests." I also printed trifold brochures detailing our commitments to the environment, community, and personal health and had them all placed at the entrance to a café at a busy corporate campus.

During a focus group of frequent café guests, I started by asking if they were interested in corporate social responsibility, environmental protection, nutrition, and so forth. "Yes," most people said enthusiastically. I then asked if anyone had seen the information we had put out. The room fell silent. "That big sign at the café entrance?" I prompted. Nothing. "With the Circle of Responsibility?" One woman finally said, "Oh, I saw that, but I thought if I read it, I'd have responsibility for something. I've already got enough responsibility."

I had created a sign for me, based on my way of thinking, my program name, my motto. I had forgotten a crucial thing: the needs of our customers.

Sometimes people are surprised by how much I focus on PR and marketing sustainability, but I believe it's crucial. Telling an engaging story about your efforts is one of the most important aspects of getting sustainability right—right up there with backing up your sustainability commitments. You deserve credit for what you're doing, and the more people know, the more others will want to participate. The goal is not just to be more sustainable but to be a brand known for it and to create a ripple effect spurring others to also make change.

This isn't always easy, and some of my advice will even sound contrarian, but you must commit to doing it well or it will backfire. You'll either end up being ineffective, like I was with my campaign, or worse, you'll be seen as straight up greenwashing. You must become an expert storyteller so people appreciate your efforts and give you credit in the marketplace for being more sustainable than your competitors. Tell the story that people want to hear, and they will listen.

To move from a company that does good work to a company that's *known* for its good work, tell your story through many channels. The unique challenge presented when building a brand around sustainability is to balance being scientifically accurate, understandable for your customers, and newsworthy. You'll need to invest in making sure every person at your company has the corporate commitments down cold, that they know the facts behind your efforts. Your framework for your company's ethos must be digestible, repeatable, and inspiring. All the conviction in the world won't matter if you can't grab people's attention.

Follow these four steps to effectively tell your story and avoid mistakes like I made by creating a poster that my customers avoided reading:

Step one: Get your story straight. Word choice and delivery matter. First, make sure you and your people truly understand the vocabulary and use words correctly, for both clarity of message and precision of science. This will establish credibility for your brand.

Step two: Craft an engaging campaign, one that will resonate with customers.

Step three: Practice your elevator pitch, keynote, and podcast interview. Always be ready to deliver your powerful message verbally with confidence (that's right, it's time to polish your public-speaking skills). Tell your story often and in as many ways as possible.

Step four: Embrace PR in all its forms. Make your story part of the public discourse through a diverse PR campaign, one that doesn't rely on others to explain what makes you special.

Let's get into it.

Step One: Get Your Story Straight

If you want your brand to be known for sustainability, everyone in your organization must be able to tell your story, including explaining scientific terms and weaving a heartwarming tale that brings your brand to life.

At Bon Appétit, I invested a huge amount of time and resources in teaching our people the science and the thought processes behind our commitments so that they knew not only what our policy was and how to operationalize it, but why we made certain decisions. Every salaried employee throughout the company—every chef, manager, controller, marketing assistant, and so on—had to complete fourteen online trainings covering topics such as local purchasing, food and climate change, sustainable seafood, and nutrition. To reach the frontline staff, we created scripts for managers to deliver during the prelunch service-staff meetings called 10@10s (10 minutes at 10 a.m.).

One of the most popular tools for 10@10s was an oversize deck of flashcards with questions on one side and answers on the other so managers could quiz staff, create trivia games, and always have a quick lesson ready. A session might start with a chef asking for volunteers to read aloud a card with the definition of a Farm to Fork vendor (owner operated, under $5 million in sales, and 150 miles from the kitchen). A catering attendant reads in English, then a barista recites the information in Spanish, as the cards have both languages. Then the group is asked to name one of that specific café's Farm to Fork partners. Sometimes shy at first, once one brave person shouts out a name like "Horse Listeners Orchard!" and gets a round of applause from their coworkers, the cooks, cashiers, and supervisors often get competitive, proudly listing local farm after local farm.

This foundational training was reinforced with a monthly all-company webcast I hosted with expert speakers, followed by a lively Q&A. The most popular sessions were Ask Me Anything, featuring our CEO or president. Our people most often wanted to know about how the Bon Appétit Dream (the company mission statement) was impacted by fiscal responsibility. This presented an opportunity for senior leaders to reaffirm their commitment to our values and explain how living up to our sustainability commitments should be seen as a revenue driver, not merely an expense.

For our executives, I went even further. During sales presentations, quarterly business reviews, town halls, and even student-government meetings, our district managers and regional vice presidents were put in the position of needing to explain our sustainability commitments to potential or current clients, customers, and other important stake-holders. Representing our company in their communities, they had to be able to speak accurately and persuasively. My mindset was that our countless hours of research and millions of dollars spent on more-ethical food that differentiated Bon Appétit could be erased in five minutes by a district manager misspeaking or even BS-ing in a sales presentation. So we put together a daylong public-speaking boot camp and took it on the road. Experts went topic by topic, breaking down the science of a broad range of subjects from antibiotic resistance to biodegradable packaging to food's contribution to climate change and more. They were well versed in Bon Appétit's policy on each issue and, most importantly, the talking points the leadership team needed to become pros at saying out loud.

After each expert presented a topic, participants were asked to get up in front of their peers and give a short talk on the subject. While a few were confident and jumped at the chance to practice their spiels, many of the executives were terrified. There were shaky voices, trembling hands, and sweaty shirts. In Minneapolis, a district manager who had done a great job signing up Farm to Fork vendors in his area and speaking to clients one-on-one was so scared to speak that he left the room in tears before his turn. I gave him time to gather himself, checked in with him, and reviewed his note cards, assuring him he had the right information at the ready. I encouraged him to tell a story about visiting farmers Ben Doherty and Erin Johnson at New Creations Farm, which he had done many times, and he was able to fumble through a short talk in front of the group. His peers cheered his triumph of trying, and he finished the session having chipped away at a deep-seated fear.

By the end of the day, all had made progress, but it was clear not everyone was ready for prime time. This was valuable information for me: I knew who to direct future interviews to, ask to attend community meetings, or speak at sales presentations.

This type of training is even more critical for mission-driven companies. If your organization's entire reason for existing is to create a more sustainable economy, any hint that you're not expert on the subject will cast doubt on your motives. You must be exact in your wording: something as seemingly straightforward as your price list can undermine your company's credibility. A misused term, even on an order sheet, shows a lack of basic understanding of the issues. I often saw companies seeking to supply us fall into this trap. One food distribution startup that was genuinely doing needed work to reduce waste showed a remarkable deficiency of knowledge. Their price sheet, for example, offered two different brands of chicken, one highlighted as "raised without hormones." The other made no mention of hormones. Many people would draw the obvious conclusion that the first company was raising their chickens more sustainably because they weren't using added hormones. However, the FDA doesn't allow the use of artificial or added hormones in poultry production. When I asked the vice president of external affairs about what I saw as a mistake, she said they merely listed the product attributes their vendors had given them. One listed "no hormones" and the other didn't. To me, this was a red flag. What else didn't they understand about the food system they were claiming to improve?

I offered this company an informal Language of the Food Movement class to improve their ability to showcase the work they're doing, without ringing alarm bells from their customers who are fluent in sustainability issues. We spent an intense day breaking down the issues and available certifications for animal welfare, sustainable seafood, and farmworkers' rights to build mastery of the products they were selling. I recorded the session and used the presentations as further training for my own team.

As you may have figured out, I'm fanatical about the power of words both to build your brand and to erode it. This should serve as fair warning to any person interested in selling something to me that is poorly or inaccurately described that you're going to get an earful, or even be subjected to a multihour training.

But that's how you become a brand built on sustainability, not just one that likes to say they're doing sustainable stuff in their ads. Be obsessive about your brand's story. Commit to the ongoing task of getting your story straight. Bake your story into the onboarding and training processes. Invest in building fluency throughout your organization or risk your own people undermining your company's reputation.

Step Two: Craft a Persuasive Campaign

Here comes the harder task: distilling all that complex information down to a digestible marketing campaign that will resonate with your customers, partners, the press, and all the other stakeholders who are vital to your company's success.

At this point you should have fallen in love with the nitty-gritty details (I instructed you to do earlier in this book). You'll want to tell everyone who will listen the difference between gestation crates and farrowing crates in pork production, or how fish-aggregating devices harm juvenile fish. I certainly did. And I've just told you how important it is to spend hours giving every member of your team a huge amount of information. Your customers, though, don't want to spend hours learning about your product. They want to quickly assess if it's aligned with what's important to them: the classic "What's Important to Me?" perennially taught in marketing classes.

Remember that big Circle of Responsibility board I put up at the entrance to a café, the one that people universally ignored? I'd focused on all the details that were important to me, not our guests. In trying to show that Bon Appétit was taking responsibility for our impact on the food system, I'd inadvertently implied our guests had responsibilities they didn't want to carry.

What turned around that campaign was advice from one of the focus group attendees, who said, "It's really about knowing what you're eating. That's what the sign should say." He was right. Guests wanted to know what they were eating, not what Bon Appétit had taken responsibility for. They wanted to know what was in it *for them*.

I started observing customers. When people entered the café, they were in a hurry, hungry, and had no time to stop to pick up a brochure—plus what would they do with it while they grabbed their food? I hadn't walked in their proverbial shoes. I was so focused on delivering the information I wanted them to have, I hadn't considered what or how they wanted to receive it.

The Circle of Responsibility board was replaced with one that said, "Know What You're Eating," while bullet points replaced the brochures. It was a step in the right direction, but busy guests still didn't take the time to stop at the café entrance and read the list. Eventually, I distilled the campaign to a standing banner at the entrance of the café that changed seasonally and featured a beautiful big photo of a farm or fresh produce and a few words aimed at communicating one broad idea like "Fresh: Bursting with Flavor and Nutrients . . . Bon Appétit." I added table tents (printed cards folded into self-standing tents) with a bit more detail, including online resources. One of my proudest marketing moments was when a guest quoted the messaging from a table tent back to me during the Q&A portion of a lecture I was giving. I'd finally succeeded at getting someone to read our materials.

Through many efforts and errors, I've learned that lunch is a terrible time to try to teach someone anything, whether or not manure is involved. At Bon Appétit, we fed college students and corporate employees. If they made time to get away from their desks or class to sit down for a meal, the last thing they wanted to do was learn. They wanted to catch up with friends, text, look at social media, play online chess, just zone out—anything but learn! A meal is a break from a busy day, a respite; it's not the time to read about human trafficking in the tomato fields or the collapse of commercial fishing.

Any industry will be the same. When creating your communication, think about when and where people will *want to* receive that kind of information. For example, checking out at a grocery store is probably not the best time to market your packaging practices—people are trying to get a bunch of food into bags without breaking their eggs and get home. (Chef David Kinch from Manresa Restaurant has a lot of opinions about when and how customers are primed to hear a story. Read about them in our interview on page 212.)

I discovered that the key to getting most people to be receptive to hearing about sustainability is prepping them for a celebration or special event. For example, even though we'd been buying locally for years and had Farm to Fork labeling in place along with marketing collateral, our guests didn't really take notice until I created the Eat Local Challenge. The initiative was inspired by a 2005 *San Francisco Chronicle* article about Jessica Prentiss and three other Bay Area women trying to eat a one-hundred-mile diet. Jessica described the group as "locavores," coining the term that would become part of the food movement's lexicon. I knew Bon Appétit customers couldn't eat 100 percent locally all the time at our cafés, but we could "go all the way" for one day and really show our guests the breadth of what was available right around them. We served an entire meal made of ingredients from within 150 miles of the café, the only exception being salt. Since it was a one-day event, we promoted it heavily, and people came to the café primed for something different to be happening. They arrived ready to receive.

Our chefs created meals that showcased the beauty and deliciousness of local food. Farmers came to the cafés and interacted with people who had planned for longer lunch breaks in anticipation of this special event. Several guests said we should buy locally all the time, showing me they'd missed all the local items that were in the café every single day. I call this the Dorothy Syndrome: like Dorothy in the *Wizard of Oz*, people need a tornado of an interruption to open their eyes to what has been there all along.

I also learned over time that to be most effective, a campaign should be positive. For the first Eat Local Challenge in 2005, I focused the marketing on the loss of biodiversity caused by the industrialized food system. I had posters of an apple with a sticker saying, "I'm the last of my kind" alongside stats about dwindling numbers of apple varietals. I noted that eye-opening study about the average food in the United States traveling 1,500 miles to its plate accompanied by an image of a stalk of broccoli with a little suitcase. No, I'm not kidding. I'm sharing these embarrassing attempts at marketing using sad fruits and vegetables in hopes of preventing you from repeating my mistakes.

Luckily for me, the incredible local-food spread put out by our chefs was more memorable than my silly graphics, and the Eat Local Challenge was a huge success. Guests left the café that day with full bellies, feeling more connected to the farmers in their communities, having had a lunch worth bragging about. Customers told friends about the meal, making our story their story.

People want to feel good about consuming your product, not have it remind them of all the ills of the world. This is tricky with sustainability because being a leader requires taking on issues that haven't hit the mainstream, so we felt we needed to explain the problem for the customer to appreciate how we were trying to solve it. Why would anyone care that we didn't buy chickens raised without the routine use of antibiotics—if they didn't even know antibiotics were used in industrial animal husbandry as a growth promoter, or what a threat antibiotic resistance is to public health?

But telling customers about a global health crisis created by antibiotics doesn't get people excited to learn more about your brand. At a certain point, our marketing campaigns resembled an inventory of threats to humanity (your food choices are contributing to climate change, animals are being kept in tiny cages, we're breeding superbugs) with a short mention at the end that we don't buy products that do whatever awful thing we just described in detail. I call it "The Sky Is Falling Marketing," and we know what happened to Chicken Little. Nobody bought her product.

Figuring out how to focus on the sunny side was, frankly, tough for me at first. But the answer came when I stopped thinking about the information I thought customers needed and instead focused on the *feeling* I wanted them to have. I wanted guests to *feel proud* of themselves and their choices. This led to our most popular campaign: "You're Already Doing Something Great." It covertly covered our work around climate change, supporting local food systems, and farmworkers' rights—just without the tired guilt trip. It put the diner at the center rather than our company. Our good work became their good work. While the campaign was initially aimed at creating warm and fuzzy feelings for our guests, our own employees swelled with pride when they read the materials, and they asked to use them beyond the cafés at community Earth Day celebrations, recruiting events, and other informational fairs.

A successful campaign that makes people feel good will permeate your entire company's culture, from your brand reputation to employee satisfaction. Avoid the sky-is-falling mentality and instead craft your message in the positive.

But don't get too cute and obfuscate your message. This is another common pitfall. You don't want guests to have to do mental gymnastics to figure out what you're trying to tell them. For our first campaign promoting compostable to-go containers made from polylactic acid derived from corn, we came up with a cute tagline about "corn not oil" and left guests befuddled instead of excited. Turned out most people don't know conventional plastic is a petroleum product, and what we thought was a fun play on corn oil just wasn't.

A more straightforward message highlighting corn as a renewable resource (a positive!) was more effective. Eventually, that gave way simply to stickers on the packages that said "compostable" as people just needed the benefit, not the details that made it possible. When you draft a campaign, be clear, not clever.

To help customers mentally organize the main message of your campaign, simplify the information by putting it into a digestible framework. A long list of seemingly disparate commitments is overwhelming, and people can't grasp the impact. At Bon Appétit, for example, we grouped all messages under community, environment, and personal well-being. If your brand is totally environmentally focused, you might bucket your policies under land, sea, and air. That way, even the most casual customer knows you've got everything covered, and the more interested customers can dig in if they want to learn that "land" encompasses actions you've taken to build soil health, combat deforestation, and protect greenspaces in the community; "sea" includes sustainable seafood as well as preventing water pollution and plastic waste; and "air" focuses on reducing climate impacts and air pollution from factory farming. You're giving people a way to make sense of your good actions.

I was once asked to help a leading consumer packaged goods company determine the next area of sustainability they should take on to connect with customers. Their sustainability team took me through what they'd already accomplished. Most of their ingredients had some sort of certification, but not the same one; they were using trains rather than trucks for more climate-friendly distribution; they had a project aimed at regenerative agricultural practices and another for preserving pollinators; they were trialing a pilot program to recycle their packaging; the list went on and on.

My reaction was twofold. First, "Wow! You're doing so many things!" As a customer who cares about these issues, it was an impressive list. Their corporate commitment was real and deep. My second reaction was, "You're doing so many things!" Even as a customer who cares about these issues, I had no idea they had taken so many actions. How could all these seemingly unrelated actions be communicated to their customers? It was too much to digest. My suggestion wasn't that they do more; it was that they figure out a schema to communicate what they were already doing.

Chipotle does this well with their "For Real" campaign. Instead of a laundry list of policies, they bucket their commitments as "Real Ingredients. Real Purpose. Real Flavor." Even if guests don't read beyond that tagline, they quickly get a message about the food (ingredients), the company (purpose), and what's in it for them (flavor). Those who take the time to dig deeper learn about Chipotle's Certified Humane pork, food donations, a debt-free degree program for employees, and much, much more. There are impressive stats—Chipotle is purchasing over 40.7 million pounds of organic and transitional ingredients and achieving a 50 percent landfill diversion rate, but that's not where their marketing materials start.[1] They start with a simple, positive message—For Real!

To craft an effective marketing campaign that communicates the amazing work you're doing and resonates with your customers, don't miss the forest for all the trees that you're saving: keep your message simple, clear, and positive.

Step Three: Start Talking

A well-crafted print and digital marketing campaign will tell your brand's sustainability story, but it pales in comparison to the impact of a well-delivered presentation. Create as many opportunities to talk about your brand as you can. This can be on a scale as grand as a talk at the venerable South by Southwest (SXSW) conference in Austin, Texas, or as small as a meeting with a single potential investor. It could be with a general-interest audience or with a specific reporter interviewing you for a story on a single effort you've taken. When you start looking for them, you'll find endless occasions to speak about your brand.

Are you already feeling nervous about speaking in front of a group? You're not alone. When I first started giving talks, I can remember thinking I'd rather die than get up in front of the group, or more specifically, I might die when I got up in front of the group or at least pass out. I spoke as quickly as possible to get the darn thing over with. I once gave a five-minute speech in just two minutes and thirty seconds. It was like I was verbally outrunning the Grim Reaper.

Giving a talk about sustainability, on any scale, brings additional complications. You're talking about politically charged subjects, ones that may spark passion in you and your audience, and complex science—all potentially making it hard to get the right words out. Add to that the possibility that you might be speaking to activists or skeptics, entrenched in their way of thinking or cynical about a for-profit company caring about the topic.

I promise you that public speaking, even to an audience of skeptics, gets easier with repetition and preparation. There is no substitution for simply getting up and doing it again and again, but there are some things you can do to ease the pain and amplify your impact. Here are my tips from having presented on sustainability hundreds of times to everyone from stoic businesspeople in China to angry environmental clubs on college campuses. They'll serve you well whether you're presenting to your board of directors, at an all-hands meeting, or even just a single disgruntled customer.

When things get hot, remember your goal. I'm never trying to convince anyone that my supply chain is 100 percent clean or to completely change someone's mind about a topic they care deeply about. My goal is for my audience to walk away thinking Bon Appétit is run by thoughtful people who ground their decisions in science. It's unrealistic to think people will agree with everything I've done, but I hope they'll see that, while we may disagree, each decision was made after research and serious consideration.

I faced inevitable disagreement when called on to speak to a group of activist students at Evergreen State College. And by "disagreement," I mean idealistic eighteen-year-olds called me names while I calmly listened to them. The group was upset that another company owned by Bon Appétit's parent company was feeding soldiers during the Iraq War. As they saw it, the money they spent at our cafés on their Olympia, Washington, campus supported a company that was war profiteering.

The only acceptable solution in their eyes was for the college to operate its own food service and even to grow its own food. This was not the first time a group of Evergreen Geoducks, so called for their school mascot, had demanded that a food-service company be thrown off their campus. I was told that, as an act of protest, students had even taken the managers with the previous provider hostage.

I knew the school administrators were not interested in going "self-op," the industry term for an organization that runs its own dining facilities. I also knew I wasn't going to convince these students that defense contracting is moral. My goal for speaking to them was to defuse the situation by listening to their concerns and showing them that we weren't "the Man," but instead regular people who were like-minded in many ways.

I was warned by our local team not to wear clothing with logos or display other tells that I was part of the establishment, as that might trigger more conflict, so I put on my proverbial big-girl pants and an awkward outfit of a plain white T-shirt, ill-fitting but unbranded pants I found in the back of my closet, and vegan leather shoes and joined the group sitting on the floor in a circle.

Things started off hot. One student branded me "an evil weapon of war" and was met with finger-snaps of support from his peers. It was shocking, but I didn't lose my cool. I went back to my goal: to show these students that we were real people who cared deeply about many of the same issues they were passionate about. I refrained from responding directly to the accusation and let student after student describe the food system they wished to see.

"That's an incredible vision, and we'll do everything we can to help you get there, even though the eventual result will be us losing your business," I finally replied. "While you're not ready for food sovereignty yet, how about I connect you with students at St. Olaf College who have started an organic farm on campus? We buy everything they can grow and serve it all in the café. I can also arrange for our Farm to Fork vendors to be on campus for a farmers' market, so you can see who we're supporting, and also buy directly from them."

I could feel the room calm as I continued offering up ideas for what we could do together. The student who called me a name even apologized for his "violent act." We'd never meet their desire to unhook from the industrial food system, but that wasn't my goal. They did now see that Bon Appétit wasn't just old white men guarding their war chests. I wasn't as different from them as they'd imagined (although they had a lot more gear with logos than I did). Goal satisfied!

To effectively engage with audiences of all sizes, from speaking events to client meetings, have a clear understanding of your goal beforehand. Keep this aim front of mind and create a prompt to remember it when you feel things getting uncomfortable so you can navigate more-emotional topics with greater confidence.

Remember to share imperfections because they make your story more authentic. Instead of making sweeping statements about how fantastic our policies are, I'll often talk about the struggles I went through to create and implement a standard. Include your challenges and missteps to make your talk more interesting and relatable, and your message more instructive.

For example, here's an excerpt from a speech I made:

> I, like many of you, read the *Guardian* article about fishermen trafficked into slavery and was horrified. The difference between you and me might be that I oversee, among other things, the seafood purchases of a $1.5 billion company. I immediately moved into action. I called our tuna, shrimp, and white fish suppliers. I lobbied Seafood Watch to add a social dimension to their ratings. I went, uninvited, to an ILO conference in Bali. I spoke alongside Greenpeace on the subject at the SeaWeb Solutions Summit in Malta. I asked questions of aquaculture industry executives in Vietnam and China. I met with formerly enslaved Burmese migrants in Thailand.
>
> I've talked, I've asked, I've prodded, I've implored. What I haven't done is offer any assurance that there is no slavery taking place in our supply chain. I do think I've created more awareness and signaled to the seafood industry that large buyers care about people working on boats and in processing plants, but that article came out in 2014 and I stand here today still unable to tell you confidently that our supply chain is clean.

Notice how I start my speech with a list of things I've done to show that I'm honestly trying to make a difference. The audience assumes I'll next launch into my list of accomplishments. When I pivot to my failings, I'm endeared to a room of newly active listeners. They're curious why I'm telling them about my struggles, and what it means for their future.

If you admit to fears, foibles, and failings, people will trust you're telling the truth about your successes and accomplishments, and they'll be more captivated by your story.

Tell stories to break up a dense list of policies. Transport your audience to a farm, factory, or even conference room through describing your surroundings and your feelings. Use all five senses. Here's another excerpt:

> As I walked through row after row of laying hens stacked in cages, my eyes stung from the ammonia in the air, and I jumped with fright every time a chicken squawked setting off a cacophony of hundreds of birds calling out.

or

> I stood in front of the board of directors knowing I had a message to deliver that they weren't going to like and tried to stop my voice from trembling.

Paint a picture and share emotion to captivate your audience, build authenticity, and make your talk more memorable. People don't retain dates and numbers, but they do remember stories.

Make people laugh when it's appropriate. Often my stories use humor, and frequently, crucially, I'm the butt of the joke. I try to break down barriers between me and the audience and come across like a human being, not a corporate automaton. I tell the story about the time I was in Kochi, India, at a seafood conference and the heel of my shoe got caught on the trade show floor and broke off just before I had to meet with the Marine Products Export Development Authority as the sole representative of the US food-service industry demanding more sustainable shrimp-farming practices. Clumsily acting out how I hobbled into the room while trying to look authoritative helps win over an audience expecting the same old corporate platitudes and empty promises from a businessperson. It's also a great way to show my level of commitment to these issues. It shows I'll travel across the world and put myself in awkward positions for important issues.

If you have a funny story about a lighthearted subject, don't be afraid to use it—and bonus points if it leans toward gentle self-deprecation.

Be careful what you speak lightly about. Humor can be a valuable tool to engage your audience, but it's not appropriate in every situation. Never talk about the suffering of people or animals in jest. This is not the place for dark humor or dry sarcasm. Know your audience. If you're talking to a group of animal welfare activists, the sacred cows may be literal.

Vary your tone as the subjects you're talking about change. In general, you'll be more engaging if you have a smile in your voice. Positivity is attractive. Just be sure to drop the brightness, and maybe even lower your voice an octave, when covering serious issues. The change of tone will signal to the audience that you understand the gravity of issues like climate change and are working hard on minimizing your company's impacts.

Watch the pace of your language when you're talking about very serious subjects. Slow down and let the words sink in. I like to use well-placed pauses to let the audience really feel the weight of what I'm saying. I write them into my speeches:

> Florida has been called "Ground Zero for modern-day slavery" by one federal prosecutor. [pause]
>
> I'm not being dramatic like, "I work so hard. I'm a slave to my job." [Put back of hand to forehead and tilt head back in a pseudo dramatic motion.]

I'm talking about people . . . [pause]

actually being enslaved . . . [pause]

locked in box trucks . . . [pause]

being forced to work without pay.

Their families threatened if they escape.

It's important to not rush through these shocking details, and intentionally planning those breaks allows people to process the severity of my words.

On the other hand, you can also purposefully speak quickly in some situations. You may choose to speed up your pace to show that you're in a flurry of activity, that things are coming fast and furious, or that they're confusing. You can throw out lots of scientific terms very quickly to illustrate how disorienting this stuff is. Doing this intentionally creates a visceral experience for the audience.

No one becomes a chef to worry about the difference between antibiotics, antimicrobials, ionophores, drugs important for human medicine, and those that aren't—therapeutic versus routine, prophylactic and growth-promoting! I do have a bachelor of science. [All said very quickly and then a pause here before . . .]

But it's in hotel administration! [Pause for laugh.]

Captivate your audience with not just your words, but how you say them. Use tone, pace, and timing to convey emotion.

Explain the science. Don't assume that even a highly educated audience understands the science related to your sustainability challenges. Even if they think they do, the group may have differing interpretations that lead to confusing assumptions. I often break the ice by using myself as the misinformed example.

I used to think that the problem with antibiotics use in animal production is that animals eat the antibiotics, and we eat the animals, so we're eating the antibiotics they ingest. Then, in 2002, when we partnered with the Environmental Defense Fund to write one of the first corporate policies banning the use the nontherapeutic antibiotics in chicken production, I learned that's not actually how it works. The problem isn't that we're eating antibiotics. It's that when healthy animals are constantly given low doses of antibiotics, because there's a beneficial side effect that makes them grow faster, that creates antibiotic resistant bacteria to develop that are dangerous to humans.

Then I go on to explain antibiotic-resistant bacteria, define "nontherapeutic" and other important terms, having built the case that it's OK for someone in the audience not to have known the terminology, because I, the expert, didn't either. The story allows me to neither assume nor condescend and gives me an excuse to explain a whole slew of important terms without sounding like I'm reading from a textbook.

Speak conversationally. You may be tempted to try to sound academic, as that's how we're taught smart people speak. Talk to the audience just as you would talk to a friend. Casual language encourages conversation and questions instead of a one-way lecture, and even in cases where the audience doesn't have the opportunity to reply, it's more engaging. I tend to pepper my talks with pop culture references chosen with the age of the people I'm speaking to in mind.

As a large corporation, we have a lot of power. I used to say, "With great power comes great responsibility," until I realized I was quoting Uncle Ben from *Spider-Man*.

or

Everyone's getting in on the plant-based game. Applebee's might be fancy enough for date night [start the first few moves of the viral TikTok dance done to "Fancy"], but now they've got an Impossible Burger alongside the Bourbon Steak and I bet you'll soon be able to get a plant-based Oreo Cookie Shake.

Depending on the audience and whether I'm being recorded or not, I tend to curse in speeches, too. A well-placed f-bomb wakes up the room, shows my passion, and sets me apart from the run-of-the-mill corporate speaker.

> I had reason to believe our pork supplier intentionally misled us. I told those MFers that, if it turns out I'm right and they've been lying to us, I'll tell the world. And I'll name names!

It's clear that I'm not just spouting the company line. No corporate brochure includes expletives or threats.

Dress casually. Match your approachable language with a more casual outfit. Your appearance can contribute or detract from your audience's initial read of your authenticity. I rarely suggest wearing a suit—especially for men, who should also consider skipping a tie. People in suits are perceived as being in ivory towers, not getting into the dirt (you might even be literally talking about soil) and selling things. But don't wear a flannel shirt and try to look "sustainable" if it's not who you are. Wear something that represents your personal best self.

Write out a full script. This approach is contrary to conventional wisdom about public speaking, but it will help you work out any potential bumps in your presentation. Identify the key points you want to make, the scientific terms you need to define, and the stories that are going to add color to your talk. Write out your script, read it aloud several times, and then throw it away.

Do not skip the reading-out-loud step. Some of these terms are tongue twisters. I needed to say "routine use of nontherapeutic antibiotics" many times before it easily rolled off my tongue. For my TEDx talk, I made an iPhone Voice Note of myself giving the twelve-minute speech and then recited the words along with the recording while doing the elliptical in the morning. That was extreme, but please do practice out loud, as it will help you synthesize the words.

Write out scientific words and new terms. If you're using terms that might be unfamiliar to your audience, write them out on your PowerPoint slides so that people can read them as they hear you say the word. If you're saying "recombinant bovine growth hormone" or "digital sobriety," having the terms written out can be helpful so people can catch what you're saying and not get caught up in "What did he say?" and miss the next point.

Plan an ending to leave the audience with your most powerful message. You've got to know how you're going to land this thing, or you'll wind up indicating it's over by blandly saying, "Thank you." You can do better than that. End with the myth you've busted, leave them with a bold, aspirational statement, or actively challenge the audience. End strong!

When giving a talk about combating slavery in the seafood industry, I ended by saying, "How can we be proud of protecting marine species, when we can't even protect our own?" It was a mic drop moment, and I strode off the stage leaving the audience to ponder that unflinching question. (Turned out I had one more slide I'd forgotten about. Kind of deflated the impact of the moment, but at least we all had a good laugh and I got to prove my humanity.)

Step Four: Use PR to Tell Your Story

One of my biggest PR coups was getting the company called "cheese-eating surrender monkeys" in the *Pork Network*, an influential industry trade publication. The op-ed went on to say I was "arrogantly trashing egg farmers across California and demanding that they, essentially, go out of business."

Why was this good for us? Because the insults were being hurled by a man known as Dr. Evil, Richard Berman, the man behind PR campaigns to defend cigarettes, alcohol, high-fructose corn syrup, and, in this case, industrial meat producers by discrediting activists and the sustainability-minded companies he accuses of being their puppets.[2] When an industry sics Richard Berman on you, you know you're making an impact—and the rest of the world takes notice, too.

We took that accusatory op-ed and made hay sharing it with our network of advocates, writers, customers, clients, and social media followers. I also used it as a proof point that Bon Appétit was making real change in several of my speeches to students at universities we served, industry groups, food conferences, advocates, and any potential customers I encountered in an audience. The intention of Berman may have been to discredit me, but he did the opposite.

Your PR plan's central goal is to build credibility. Of course, getting the word out about your product is also an important piece of driving sales. What is unique about the needs of a brand built on sustainability, though, is the added requirement to build authority and trustworthiness. Consumers are losing faith in the veracity of corporate claims. According to the research firm Mintel, 43 percent of millennials don't trust large food manufacturers, compared to just 18 percent of non-millennials.[3] When it comes to Gen Z, a Salesforce study found that only 42 percent said that they trust companies.[4] To get these important consumer groups to believe in the sincerity of your commitment to sustainability, it's going to take the people, press, and companies they already trust backing you.

Also, don't conflate public relations with *press* relations. Stories in traditional media outlets should be one of the tools in your PR toolbox, not the lone strategy for getting the word out to people about your sustainability actions. To tell your sustainability story, you're going to need to do just that: *tell your story*; don't rely on others to do so.

Your PR plan should include standard media pitches and press releases, opinion pieces, company-owned channels, courting of advocates, and a way to aggregate and distribute all the persuasive content you generate. The goal of this multipronged approach is to position you and your company as thought leaders who have third-party endorsements from trusted sources. Doing this well will involve taking some risks, being vulnerable, and a lot of time and effort.

Get the press to write about you. The media landscape has changed dramatically in recent years. Getting your message out can feel like you're shouting at people with earbuds in, who are listening to whichever echo chamber they prefer. There are far fewer paid reporters assigned to ever-wider beats, local papers have been gutted, and the twenty-four-hour news cycle, paradoxically, has made it harder to get coverage for smaller stories.

When I started trying to get press for Bon Appétit's sustainability initiatives, my approach was to enthusiastically tell any reporter I could get in front of about whatever great new commitment we'd made and expound on the long list of other awesome things we'd done, how sustainability was in the DNA of our company, and that we'd been at this for years. I'd then launch into a precise explanation of the science behind the change we were making and our nuanced choice of words in our policy. What I often heard in return was "Are there any other companies doing this? I need three examples to show it's a trend," or "Great, where can our readers go to your restaurants?" plus a lot of tepid "Thanks, that's nice" responses.

To get coverage, you need to create tension, take a stance, and embrace the fallout. I quickly learned I had several hurdles to overcome for Bon Appétit to be deemed worthy of press. "Company says it's good, does another good thing" isn't news. "Restaurant you can't go to changes their menu" isn't relevant to the general public. And the short attention span of today's media doesn't allow for complex explanations of science. What reporters want is quick hits of information that will create attention-grabbing headlines. In short: be interesting. You've probably heard the term "news hook," but the mistake most of us on the corporate communications side make is thinking that what's important to us, or that we've worked hard on, is news. Instead, the hook is tension. In sustainability, effective tension usually looks like taking a controversial stance that others will criticize; making a change that seems counterintuitive to business, such as greatly increasing your costs or letting people in on something that has historically been hidden from the public.

For Bon Appétit, the surprise or tension that people would write about was where you found our food: good food in unexpected places or in exclusive cafés that outsiders are not allowed to visit. Mark Bittman wrote in his *New York Times* Opinionator column about how we cook "cafeteria food that you actually want to eat, food that deserves to be served with wine."[5] Our first-of-its-kind farmstand at what was then called Pac Bell Park, home of the San Francisco Giants, garnered the headline, "A Ballpark Where Yogurt and Fresh Fruit Vie with Tradition," in the *New York Times* national edition.[6]

Letting people go behind the walls of tech giants was effective as well. CNBC called us "Silicon Valley's Hottest Player" and created additional tension in another piece through competition by asking, "Which tech company has the best free food?"[7] Those stories were Trojan horses for our sustainability messaging. We defined "hot" and "best" as using local ingredients and paying attention to the impacts of our food choices.

You can also create tension by taking an extreme stance. If done well, this tactic will bring heat, so be sure it's something you truly believe in and are willing stand up for in the face of critics. When we were the first company to talk about the connection between food and climate change, we became the punch line of a Jay Leno joke on the *Tonight Show*. I can't remember the setup, but it had something to do with farting and burritos connecting cows releasing methane gas, which they do as part of their natural digestive process, and what happens to people after they eat at Taco Bell. You can imagine the sophomoric humor. Instead of being embarrassed by being the butt of a joke, we used the mention as evidence that we were raising awareness of an important issue. When the well-respected food-advocacy news site Civil Eats wrote a story about our director of purchasing's commitment to sorting through the complexities of the seafood supply chain and her correcting one of our chefs for serving unsustainable (but very popular) bluefin tuna, *SF Weekly* followed up and called her an "eco-Nazi."[8] At first that was startling, but then we wore it as a badge of honor and used it to pitch her to other news outlets. What corporation goes so far with its commitment to sustainability that it's head of sourcing gets called an eco-Nazi? That's proof that we're taking our promises seriously.

Use a growing controversy as an opportunity to amplify your message further. This comes with a caveat: you've got to be sure you've got the stomach for it, and your communications team must be prepared to act quickly.

Back to how we got to being called "cheese-eating surrender monkeys." I submitted an op-ed to the *Des Moines Register* titled "Dear Big Ag: Stop Treating Customers Like They're Stupid," reprimanding industrial meat producers for trying to hide their practices from public view and fighting animal welfare legislation despite clear consumer support.[9] Yes, that was intentionally inflammatory, and it got their attention.

The return volley came from Derrick Sleezer—I swear I didn't make up that name—president of the National Pork Board, who called my take "misleading in its characterization of farming and uninformed on the economics" in his own opinion piece in the same publication. Things escalated as I kept responding and more people came for me. My mom called to say, "I don't think you should show your face in Iowa anytime soon!" JoAnn Alumbaugh, editor of *Pork Network* addressed us personally with an open letter, "Dear Bon Appétit: Stop pretending you're not part of the HSUS 'family.'"

I replied, "I'm not pretending. We are proud partners of the Humane Society of the United States and have been for ten years." Then I took on Randy Krotz, CEO of the US Farmers & Ranchers Alliance, a group funded by the likes of Bayer, ConAgra, and the United Soybean Board, on the syndicated radio show *The Food Chain* for an episode titled "To Know or Not Know: Who Should Control What May Be Known About Food?" All of this was time-consuming but worth the effort because it further cemented our position as a thought leader, as a company willing to take on Big Business rather than being part of the problem. It built the lore of Bon Appétit as mavericks bucking the establishment. I created the tension needed to make news.

Create tension, then build on it to get yourself the most buzz in the press. Just be sure you stand by your story.

Send press releases you know no one will write about. That's not to say you wouldn't love it if someone picked up the release and wrote a story, but don't view the action as a waste of time if no one does.

In the summer of 2021, I hired a PR agency to pitch four stories that got no traction at all: our new carbon-reduction commitment, an app-based ordering platform aimed at guests with food allergies, the 2.0 release of our sustainability reporting dashboard, and our waste-tracking tool. It was a tough news cycle, with the pandemic still dominating. I'd hoped that together, our four releases would add up to a surprising, tension-filled story, something like "In the face of almost total business shutdown, Bon Appétit doesn't sway from its commitment to sustainability," but we couldn't get anyone to bite. The releases all wound up being seen as versions of "Bon Appétit is doing some more good stuff." Snoozefest! However, these were also four excuses for us to reach out to reporters and remind them about Bon Appétit or introduce ourselves to new writers. Having a reason to tell the media the company was still alive and innovating was important, even when I didn't have an article to show for it.

Build relationships with the press through a steady drumbeat of actions. Think of press releases as friendly reminders of your existence and your area of expertise. Just as with the old marketing Rule of Seven that a potential customer needs to see or hear an advertiser's message at least seven times before they'll take action to buy that product or service, repetition is needed to cement your company name in a reporter's mind. Maybe no one writes a story about our waste-tracking tool, or the previous release when we signed on to be a US Food Loss and Waste 2030 Champion, or the one before that when we put out a study on postconsumer food waste, but several months later, when a writer is looking for an expert on food waste and remembers that Bon Appétit had something to say about the subject, they'll reach out.

Since being the first to do something sustainability related is important in creating your leadership tale, every time you make or meet a commitment, send out a press release and post it on your own website. You're creating a record of your leadership.

Consciously work at being a reliable source. The press is also more likely to contact you for a story if you get back to them promptly and are prepared to deliver. A reliable source gives the writer the information they need for the story—both the context and a compelling sound bite that fits their thesis statement.

Just like your employees, writers need to be taught how to talk about the complex issues. Develop a reputation as the go-to person who can clearly explain the concerns and solutions for whatever the hot-button issues are in your industry. This may mean you have to put in a lot of time with a writer before they quote you. Over a yearlong period, I had several conversations with a Bloomberg reporter about gestation crates, Bon Appétit's policy versus other companies' policies, how raising and selling pigs differs from chickens, and the cost of higher animal welfare practices before seeing my name in print. She was trying to hone the angle of her story and needed a reliable source to hash out ideas and ground truth what other companies were telling her. I gladly played that role, hoping to make it into the prestigious business publication at some point, be it in this story or another one. When she did eventually publish a piece about businesses going back on their commitments to eliminate gestation crates, I was the only food-service company executive quoted. Better yet, she mentioned that we had eliminated the confinement systems from our supply chain.[10] The good press was clearly worth all the emails and phone calls, but even just being on the reporter's radar as an expert for a future piece would have been a valuable enough asset to justify the time spent.

The press is a customer. A reporter is only going to "buy" your story if it meets their needs. Sometimes they'll reach out researching a specific topic and other times they're in search of story ideas. Be prepared to give some stats, a great quote, or even pitch a fully formed package such as a new trend in green business with your company as one of three examples. Be sure the other examples you give aren't direct competitors of your company; you don't want to do work for your rivals. For example, if I was pitching a story on a new initiative at Bon Appétit to reduce the risk of slavery in our seafood supply chain, I would mention the work done by Thai Union (the maker of Chicken of the Sea tuna) and Costco. I'm giving the reporter three companies so it's a trend, but my examples span three parts of the supply chain: a canner, a retailer, and a food-service company.

Sometimes the reporter has an idea, and they need someone to state it on the record. That's where the art of the sound bite comes in. Most sustainability stories follow a formula. You can bet the writer will open with an attention-grabbing fact and an argument for why the topic is important. Then they'll explain the problem, what companies are doing to address it, and how this reflects a bigger trend. When you set up the interview, ask the writer a few questions to get a sense of their perspective on the subject and then plan statements that will fit into the story formula I just outlined. Help the writer move their story along by giving them the pieces you know they'll need, using catchy language. Build your sound bite; don't just hope it's going to come out naturally in conversation. Then, no matter what they ask you, find an opportunity to repeat (or counter) the writer's thesis succinctly and interestingly. Most good reporters will ask a softball question at the end of the interview that is some version of "What have I not asked that you think I should know?" Or, you can always say, "I'd like to add . . ." Repeat your sound bites with emphasis. Do this one of three ways:

1. *State the thesis:* "The most shocking fact is that people are being killed in an effort to bring us low-cost tuna."

2. *Explain the problem:* "The biggest hurdle to ensuring seafood supply chains are free from slavery is the number of times seafood changes hands before reaching our restaurants."

3. *Highlight the trend:* "Now that slavery in seafood has been exposed, the public is going to demand more transparency and assurance from food companies just as they did with sweatshops and sneakers."

Make it easy for the reporter. Give them what they need and you're sure to make it into the story.

Don't forget smaller media outlets. I'm name-dropping the *New York Times* and Bloomberg, but you don't always have to go after the big media fish. A press hit in a local paper that everyone in your target community reads may be as effective in building your company's reputation, or more effective, with potential customers than a national media outlet that's seen in markets in which you don't operate.

We utilized the same techniques of creating tension and being great sources on smaller-scale stories in local TV and newspapers by creating an event highlighting an unexpected meal in a place most people don't get to see and providing fantastic photo ops, another version of the sound bite. Our Eat Local Challenge was a perennial news-getter in the likes of the *Newark Advocate, Northfield News,* and *East Bay RI,* plus the local TV affiliates who would show up, especially when our farmers brought a few of their animals along or set up colorful produce displays. (Pitching many small regional outlets is time-consuming, though, so we taught our local teams to pitch themselves and armed them with customizable press packets.)

Local news is an effective way to reach a specific community or create fodder for your newsletters (more on your newsletters coming). I once brimmed with excitement after seeing our online Low

Carbon Diet Calculator featured live on CNN—I was sure traffic to the site would skyrocket. Checking our Google Analytics after the story broke showed only three hundred visitors that day, hardly a windfall. Don't make my mistake of overestimating the power of big press, nor should you underestimate the potential of small stories. Focus on all the avenues that are available to you.

Write your own story via op-eds and contributed columns. A story in the *New York Times* or *Wall Street Journal* is still the brass ring in PR. Both papers are widely read and seen by many as some of the last bastions of objective reporting. However, even if you can get into those lauded papers, they might not write the exact story you hoped for. Remember that *New York Times* story on farm-fresh food in ballparks I proudly presented earlier? It left our name out of the piece! We were referred to only as "the same caterers as the Getty Center in Los Angeles." As crushed as I was, the story was still useful: it drummed up more business for the farmstand, it made our clients the Giants happy, and we shared the piece widely, adding the context that the menu had been our idea and we were running the stand. However, it would've been better if our name was prominently featured, and our critical role highlighted. You can ensure you're positioned to your liking by doing the writing yourself through op-eds and contributed columns.

You cannot, however, just write an op-ed about how great your company is and how many sustainability commitments it has. Opinion editors aren't in the business of letting for-profit companies write free advertorials. They are, however, interested in an insider's view and executives willing to take an unpopular stand or elucidate in a simple way a complex idea people are struggling with.

Keep an eye on news related to the issues you care about and jump when you see an announcement or other opinion piece you disagree with. Yes, disagree. The only op-ed of support that will get published is if you support legislation that seems counter to your company's interests. For example, say you're a major egg supplier who is supporting a proposition requiring cage-free production that would mandate you to make expensive changes to your farms, or a janitorial company with many minimum-wage workers that is supporting the fight for a living wage. The need for tension remains important when pitching op-eds.

To get an op-ed published, see an issue, craft a short, punchy opinion piece within twenty-four to forty-eight hours, and submit to the outlet in which you saw the original news. Or, if you're responding to a big story, submit to the place you think will be most intrigued by your take.

In addition to traditional newspapers' opinion pages and letters to the editor, many online publications are hungry for content creators who will work for little or no money, bring their own audience, and speak with authority. Over the years, I've had regular columns at the *Huffington Post* and *Forbes*, both brand-name outlets with reputations that served as proof points that what I say can be trusted. Since Bon Appétit was paying me, I was able to write for free, our large customer base brought the publications to new readers, and I had a track record of both business expertise and being vocal. Just as with an op-ed, contributed columns can't be obviously about your company. You need to write about something happening in the news, then comment on the issue from the perspective of a food company executive. This usually looks something like, "Oh, and by the way, I know a lot about this because my own company has led the industry on this issue." Have strong opinions, back them up, and write about them while the topic is still hot.

Work with advocacy groups. The best endorsement you can get is from an advocacy group known for criticizing businesses. A positive mention from an activist organization like Greenpeace or PETA carries weight. This is the one area of PR where "look at all the good we're doing!" is welcome and will garner attention. Groups like the Humane Society are eager to highlight corporate wins in hopes of inspiring others to make similar changes.

Still, a story with tension will get more attention. When World Animal Protection released its first *Quit Stalling* report ranking how well food companies were doing on honoring their commitments to end the use of gestation crates, Bon Appétit's score was fine. We were placed in the yellow category—one under green, the highest level, and above the orange, pink, and red tiers. I didn't think just being listed in the rankings was an accurate reflection of the efforts we made to be leaders on the issue though, so I suggested a case study on how, due to Covid-19-related business interruptions, we'd missed our 2021 target but redoubled efforts and would be in compliance by the end of 2022. Pointing out that we didn't live up to a public commitment left us vulnerable to criticism but also made the story interesting. The next *Quit Stalling* report featured a full page titled "Bon Appétit Stands Firm on Sow Welfare Despite Unprecedented Challenges." No other company got that much ink. Not even the ones with the highest scores.

Don't walk on eggshells with advocacy groups. Be interesting! Find the tension that will get the advocacy groups to advocate for you.

Use social media, blogs, and loyalty programs to build engagement. Few people are going to peruse your company blog, your customers outside Iowa aren't going to see your remarks in the *Des Moines Register*, and only people in the pork industry follow *Pork Network*. These are not big communications victories in themselves, but they are more ammo. To make them effective in getting the word out, you'll need to republish the content somewhere else.

When we tangled with Rick Berman, aka PR's Dr. Evil, in that obscure publication, we tweeted it out and tagged the Humane Society so it and all its 800,000 followers who care about farm animal welfare would see it:

> Acc to Rick Berman, @bamco = "cheese-eating surrender monkeys" for caring about hens & pigs (& listening to @HSUS)

While Bon Appétit doesn't have a huge number of followers, we are watched by several key people. We consciously courted "the choir," writers and influencers who agreed with our stance on sustainability.

Since the purpose of this communications strategy is to build credibility, aim to make sure those critical endorsers tune in. They're the most likely to report on our actions and the most trusted by those cynical customers we're trying to win over.

Create a way to speak directly to your most engaged customers. Be it a loyalty program, a coupon in exchange for allowing text messaging, or a special designation like Chipotle's Burrito Ambassadors, you need to invest in a relationship with turbo users of your brand and then share these stories with them directly. At Bon Appétit, we put out a *Quarterly Sustainability Highlights* newsletter that went to our clients, guests who signed up on our café websites, a curated media list, and all our advocacy partners. Each season we sent out a news roundup with pretty pictures, infographics, and quotes from the press about us and some of our own blog content.

Use all these channels in concert: a press release next to an op-ed next to a highlight from an advocacy group, topped with a blog entry, social media post, and a newsletter. When an interested reporter or a doubting customer comes to criticize, your blog post from 2015 showing you were the first to do this really cool thing will rebuff them. Build a solid communications structure that positions you as the trusted expert in your field, and the word will get out.

ACTION ITEMS

How to Tell Your Story

To level up from a company that's not just doing good work, but one that's *known* for doing good work, you must become an expert in telling your story.

Strike the delicate balance between being scientifically accurate while also crafting a narrative that is easy to understand and newsworthy by following these four steps:

Step one: Get your story straight. Invest in ensuring that every-one at your organization, at every level, can tell your story with confidence and accuracy.

Step two: Craft a persuasive campaign. Distill all the complex details into digestible marketing materials that will resonate with a variety of audiences.

Step three: Start talking. Polish your public-speaking skills and create as many opportunities as possible to speak about your brand live.

Step four: Use PR to tell your story. Take a multipronged approach, employing traditional media pitching, writing op-eds, courting advocates, and using company-owned chan-nels to build both credibility and engagement. Garner attention by creating tension, taking a stance, and embracing the fallout. Sustainability is not for the faint of heart.

Interview

Picking Your Spots
with Storytelling

DAVID KINCH
Chef and owner, Manresa Restaurant

As the chef and owner of Manresa restaurant in Los Gatos, California, David Kinch earned three Michelin stars, the highest rating in the culinary world, along with a reputation for his commitment to local sourcing. His groundbreaking relationship with Love Apple Farms helped launch a trend of farms growing solely for a single restaurant, the chef and farmer working hand in hand to craft bespoke ingredients.

But, just like Bon Appétit's commitment to buying locally, Manresa's decision started as a culinary act, not a political one. That's remained true for David, a bit of nonconformist who eschews the now-standard farm-to-table fable in favor of simply putting great food on the plate yet has found himself drawn into the conversation about the ethics of food by a rising tide of interest from his peers and customers.

Though David thinks about storytelling in terms of what is presented at a restaurant table, never mind the industry you're in, the themes he hits on are universal and worth thinking about with your customer-facing storytelling. Be authentic. Avoid preaching. Know what the customer wants from their experience. David is restrained in his storytelling, and therefore, the message received is all that more special.

David closed Manresa at the end of 2022. He continues to be an active partner in the restaurants Mentone and The Bywater as well as a small chain of Manresa Bread bakeries. And full disclosure, he's my significant other.

How do you approach storytelling in fine dining? On the one hand, you have this wealth of information that you could give to guests, but on the other hand, they're there to enjoy a meal.

To me, for really great fine dining, two things always had to be present. There was a common denominator at all great, ambitious restaurants, no matter where they were in the world. The first one was that the restaurant was one person's vision. It could be the chef or it could be the owner. There's one person who had a vision of what this establishment would be. It was their passion. It was a reflection of them.

The other characteristic was that the restaurant tended to be a reflection of not only who they were but *where* they were, their location. There are examples of the great restaurants of France and Italy and, to a certain extent, Spain and Japan as well. The great French country restaurants or Italian restaurants use local products. They use the wines from that particular region. You couldn't really pick this [restaurant] up and put it elsewhere, because it would seem out of place. What made it have that kind of magic was the fact that you were there and couldn't get it anywhere else.

That is all a form of storytelling.

With Manresa, we wanted to tell the story of the central coast of California. Our little special corner in the foothills of the Santa Cruz Mountains right by the Pacific Ocean. The more I cooked in this particular restaurant setting, working to create my own style with my classical background working in classical restaurants, I realized that it should be the food that does the talking.

Some restaurants do a lot of talking at the table. Does that story-telling not enhance the dining experience?

As people started to travel to unfamiliar places for fine dining, like Scandinavia and Peru, and ingredients were used that people were unfamiliar with, and chefs wanted to put themselves forward, high-light their own efforts, there had to be a spiel or this certain lecture or preaching element to the dishes where the guests were told about the dishes and maybe even how to enjoy them. "Start from the left and work your way to the right to the many different piles," as an example. "When you taste this, this is how you're going to feel. This is going to remind you of this certain part of our country," or something like this.

I think that's infantile. That's patronizing to the guests. To me that creates unnecessary expectations, maybe false expectations. If your food is good enough, and your experience is good enough, then there will be a reflection in that experience where the guests can feel that the food reflects you and your team, and where you are, without being told all of that.

A lot of people don't want that lecturing. They just want a good meal. They want to have an experience. They want to have an oasis from their frantic life and, for three hours, pay good money to escape. No cell phones, no TV, no kids, whatever it may be, to go and disappear. Some people don't want to interact with staff at all. Other people want to hear the story. Now, the art of hospitality is reading the guests and understanding the amount that's correct, but ultimately I'm just sim-ply not interested in the story, the preaching, and the political nature of fine dining. What you do is you walk the walk. You do what you believe in, and you put it on the plate, and you don't trumpet it and tell people. If they're savvy enough, or they care enough, or they're alert enough, they will see it. And to me, that's much more impactful than being given a lecture.

When you go to great lengths to get ingredients, you don't want to highlight your efforts?

It's impossible to take mediocre ingredients and make great dishes. Can't do it. Breaks the laws of physics. You know, you can have a great recipe and cook to perfection, but the way a dish is improved is by buying better-quality ingredients. It's the only way to do it.

So, I don't feel a need to brag about the fact that we make extraordinary efforts to bring in great products to the restaurant. The mantra at the restaurant was that we take great products, and we show them respect and cook them to the best of our ability to where they show themselves the best. That's what made our food special and famous to a certain extent. I feel that you can taste that on the plate.

A good example is Zuckerman Family Farms' asparagus from Sacramento. Ed Zuckerman grew a particularly large type of asparagus that I used, and then it became economically unviable for him, so he didn't offer it anymore. I went and complained and said, "I've got a small restaurant. I use you two months out of the year. I only want these big ones. Just grow the big ones for me. I'll come pick them up. I'll drive to the Ferry Building [in San Francisco, about an hour north of Manresa] and pick them up." Cultivating those kinds of relationships is key to great ingredients, but I'm big believer in letting the food speak for itself.

You served a tasting menu at Manresa and presented the guest with the menu at the end of the meal. Farm names weren't included in the descriptions, but you did list the producers on the back. What was the thinking in that choice?

To keep an element of surprise, we gave the menu at the end of the meal. Then we deliberately made the menu descriptions bland, so people really had to think about what they had to create the memory. Afterward they got just "Asparagus and Fermented Truffle." It's not "comma cuisine" where you list every single thing that's part of the dish. That was a big trend in the eighties and nineties in California, with restaurants listing every single ingredient. "Charcoal-grilled salmon with cilantro, tomato, onions, fava beans, and, and, and . . ." To me, it left nothing to the imagination. So listing the ingredients on the back of the menu on a map was so if the guest did want more information, they could see what we put together. They could see Zuckerman Family Farms there, not in midst of the menu.

As being a "foodie" became a craze, did you find that customers were asking more questions about where things came from or how they were prepared?

Guests nowadays are very, very savvy compared to a generation ago. And not only are they savvier, but they're also younger. It used to be that fine dining was a special experience saved for the rich, an elitist proposition. With the democratization of eating good food, people save their money for a special experience, and they research it. Guests know more about the ingredients, more about the people behind the food, more about different cuisines to a certain extent.

And a lot of people who came to apply to work at Manresa knew, too. I hate to say it, but it was the reputation for having a farm-to-table ethos that we'd garnered.

Why do you "hate to say" you garnered a reputation for having a farm-to-table ethos?

Because my relationship with Love Apple Farms was driven by one thing only, and that was being much more in control of the products that were entering the kitchen. California has amazing produce. It's world class. But the fact is I'd go to the farmers' markets, and I'd have three chefs in line in front of me and three chefs in back. I mean, we're all buying the same peaches, or apricots, or asparagus, or whatever. Buying directly from Love Apple was my attempt to create a degree of separation from those other chefs and to have much more control of stuff coming in. I could have things specifically grown for us. It was an exclusive relationship. It was a quality play. It wasn't a PR issue. Everything was driven by, not the politics of farm to table, but getting the best product into the restaurant.

Incidentally, by far the funniest thing I heard was, "Wow, you must be saving so much money growing your own vegetables." What they didn't realize was the relationship costs us three, four times more than it would have to just pick up the phone and call a produce company or go to the farmers' markets. I had to fight with my partners to establish that relationship.

Why did it cost three or four times more?

Who paid Cynthia's [Love Apple Farms' owner] salary? Who bought the seeds? Who paid for the labor to get things done? That was all us. It was a symbiotic relationship, but it cost the restaurant a lot of money. Delivery, maintenance, all that sort of stuff.

Perhaps the most iconic dish at Manresa was "Into the Vegetable Garden," inspired initially by the relationship with Love Apple. Is that a version of storytelling?

Absolutely. "Into the Vegetable Garden" told the story of hyperlocal, a dish made completely of ingredients from one farm. The rule of that dish was, if it was from the garden, it had to be on the plate, and if it wasn't from the garden, it could not be on the plate. Sometimes it had thirty to forty ingredients. It was a dish that changed on a daily and sometimes hourly basis as we moved through the limited quantities of each product. Ironically, it was the only dish in the restaurant's history where the wording on the menu was exactly the same the whole time. It simply said, "Into the Vegetable Garden."

How do you balance sustainability and flavor? Are there ever ingredients that you would like to use but don't because of their impacts?

I never limit myself. I never compromise the quality of ingredients. There's a couple of cases for restaurants doing that. A great example is Noma [a much-lauded restaurant in Copenhagen] in its first incarnation. It would not use anything *not* from Scandinavia. So, they eliminated olive oil. They would not use olive oil, because it wasn't from Scandinavia, and to me, that is setting up compromises. It's part of your storytelling, but it compromises how you cook and offer pleasure to the guest.

When Chilean sea bass was popular but also known to be caught unsustainably, I would not use it, because first of all, it wasn't local. And, second, there's plenty of alternatives for a firm, white, flaky fish. There are a million alternatives. But I used foie gras [flown in from France] because chicken liver pâté is not a substitute.

There are times when you do talk overtly about sustainability. You participate in World Ocean Day.

I pick my spots, and a lot of it has to do with things that are important to me and Manresa. Manresa was fish and shellfish, fruit and vegetable forward, kind of low in fat. Because of our emphasis on fish, shellfish, and seafood in general, our use of seaweeds, of being part of the Central Coast of California, doing World Ocean Day once a year is some preaching that I feel comfortable doing.

You only did it on Instagram though. There wasn't a mention in the restaurant of it, correct?

No, the restaurant's not for political acts. Restaurants are acts of hedonism and pleasure, people enjoying themselves. I don't want people crying in the restaurant.

Storytelling to Win Over Reporters, and Everyone Else

CHRIS ARNOLD

Former communications director, Chipotle Mexican Grill; vice president and head of communications, Darigold

When a friend of Chris Arnold asked him if he'd consider leaving his job at a Denver PR agency and going in-house at Chipotle Mexican Grill, he wasn't particularly interested in the food sector or the sustainable food movement. But he liked the burritos and appreciated the brand's personality. And he saw rapid growth coming for the regional chain that at the time had 120 stores, maybe an IPO, and maybe international expansion—all transitional moments that make public relations inherently more important to an organization.

What he didn't anticipate was helping build arguably the strongest restaurant brand ever based on sustainability. Chris spent fifteen years as communications director for Chipotle while it did indeed go public, expand to six countries, and grow to two thousand outlets. He now serves as vice president and head of communications for Darigold, a farmer-owned dairy cooperative in the Pacific Northwest.

How did you balance telling a complex sustainability story with meeting customers where they are?

We always thought that we had a challenging marketing and

communications problem. The things that really drove our business and that differentiated our brand were things that a lot of people, including most of our own customers, didn't really know were issues. We had to build awareness of some of the issues in large-scale food production and farming that we thought were problematic so people would then understand us as part of the solution.

How did you go about that?

We found a lot of success leveraging our farmers. When we started serving pork from Niman Ranch for our carnitas, the ingredient cost difference was significant enough that we had to raise the price of a carnitas burrito and tacos by $1, which was a huge percentage based on our price. So, we started to tell that story from the farmer's point of view. We had a very simple in-restaurant promotional campaign that included posters saying things like "We know exactly where our pork comes from: Duane," with a beautiful black-and-white portrait of a guy named Duane Dorenkamp, who was one of the Niman Ranch farmers. It told the story of this network of little family farms raising pigs in more traditional, more sustainable ways, and why we thought that was important.

But also, it fundamentally was about serving better-tasting pork, and we believed that pork raised that way tasted better and there are reasons for that. If pigs are raised in the outdoors in places like Minnesota and Iowa, they develop more back fat to protect them from the elements, and that results in a more marbled, more flavorful pork than pigs that are raised in indoor confinement. So, we told the story based on the taste and quality of the pork but also on the story of these farms.

How did the press play into your storytelling strategy?

We got a lot of play in the mainstream and the elite food press. We courted that very heavily as part of our PR strategy. At Chipotle, we took the traditional fast-food playbook entirely off the table. We weren't big advertisers. We didn't do television. We didn't do limited-time offers and that kind of discounting. We really based most of our marketing on word of mouth and things that seeded word of mouth, and we did that because we believed that people found restaurants that way. You don't find the best restaurants by watching television ads; you find them by reading restaurant reviews and asking informed friends.

We were using the same kinds of ingredients as much more expensive, much fancier fine-dining restaurants. That stuff really resonated with the food press and helped us tell a story in a way that differentiated us.

Can you give some examples?

One was in 1993, when we only had one restaurant and we got a review written by the food critic at the now-defunct *Rocky Mountain News*, one of two daily newspapers in Denver at the time. Business had been trending steadily up since Steve [Ells, founder of Chipotle] opened [the first Chipotle], but the trajectory popped way up [after the *Rocky Mountain News* review] and accelerated and held in a way that made Steve a really big believer in that kind of press and that kind of word of mouth.

Fast-forward about ten years to when we opened our first restaurant in New York, and we had a little bit of trepidation in that we were building a reputation for being this very different, sort of special kind of fast food. If we somehow disappointed the most elite food press in New York, it really stood to tarnish the reputation that we had been very deliberately cultivating.

We got a review in the *New York Times*, which was the second really notable storytelling moment for us. For a fast-food chain to get reviewed by serious food critics, particularly in the *New York Times*, was a small miracle all by itself. That we were getting reviewed favorably was much more than a small miracle.

The *Times* review started off with typical *New York Times* criticisms of chain restaurants: that they represent all that's evil in the world, the equalization of Anchorage and Akron, ironing out all the regional wrinkles that make places unique and define the character of them. But regardless of what you think about chain restaurants as a whole, Chipotle in New York serves "undeniably good food" with "forceful spicing, fresh, good-quality ingredients" and finished to order, which is an important step in the journey from something good to something that's really more extraordinary.[1] That really validated some of the things that we were thinking about marketing and PR and the core beliefs that Steve had embraced about better food and classic cooking.

Then in 2011 we had the biggest breakthrough in how we thought about and did storytelling. We made a little two-minute animated short film that we called *Back to the Start* that was set to a Willie Nelson cover of the Coldplay song "The Scientist." It traced the journey of a small farmer from more traditional sustainable farming to industrial farming and back. It was based on the story arc of a guy named Russ Kremer.

Russ ran a little co-op called Ozark Mountain Pork in a place called Frankenstein, Missouri, in the shadow of the Ozarks. He grew up on a farm family and loved pigs more than people. He went to ag school and came back and convinced the family that the only way they were going to make money in hogs was to really scale and go industrial. So they did.

Then one day, Russ, while tending to the pigs on the farm, was gored by one of his boars. The wound he suffered almost killed him. The doctors had to use one of the antibiotics of last resort to arrest the infection because it was resistant to the other antibiotics, all the antibiotics they were feeding the pigs on the farm!

Russ saw the light and said, "We're not going to do this anymore. If we're going to keep raising pigs, we're going to do it in a way that doesn't necessitate the copious use of antibiotics." So, they sold off the herd, disassembled the infrastructure, and went back to raising pigs the way they had in the past.

Back to the Start was originally intended to be a little brand-narrative film for this invitation-only loyalty program that we were developing, but we really liked it and thought more people should see it, so we put it on five thousand movie screens before the [feature] movies showed.

The response was overwhelmingly positive. So, we put it on another five thousand movie screens, and the response just got louder. Then we decided we're going to do something we never did, which was television advertising, and we ran the full two-minute film during the Grammy telecast in 2012.

Social media blew up, the common sentiment being "Chipotle's ad stole the show!" This was a show that included Whitney Houston tributes and performances by Coldplay, Paul McCartney, Adele, and a who's who of popular music at the time—and our ad stole the show. *Back to the Start* ignited a national conversation with hundreds of millions of earned media impressions and massive social media discussion.

For some time, it provided us a platform that we could keep riffing off. We'd bring people in with entertainment and then use the time that we had their attention to whip a little knowledge on them about these issues that we thought were important or make them more curious about those issues. Or we'd leverage that kind of content sometimes to create controversy, which would then force conversations in the press and across social media that put us squarely at the center of them.

We followed that with another film called *The Scarecrow* that we attached to an iPhone game, and we made a satire series called *Farmed and Dangerous* that followed the same idea and was the number two show on Hulu. Our *brand-created* show was the number two show on Hulu! These things gave us platforms. When we made *Farmed and Dangerous*, we did a big red carpet, LA premiere and had all the entertainment press there. We did a press screening in the theater room at the Bryant Park Hotel in New York; Carol Massar, the Bloomberg Television reporter, moderated a Q&A with the director and the people who made *Farmed and Dangerous* with an auditorium full of New York food and entertainment press.

When I saw *Back to the Start*, my jaw dropped. And then I immediately got a call from my CEO saying, "We should do that too!" And I said, "You're going to have to give me a much bigger budget." How did you make the leap financially from pitching stories to the

**food media to casting Coldplay and Willie Nelson, and making ads
for the Grammys?**

It wasn't as expensive as people might think. We made that film for
$400,000. So not nothing, but people spend a whole lot more to pro-
duce just a thirty-second television spot. We didn't work with ad agencies, where things tend to get sort of stupidly expensive. We hired a film
director and approached it as a little animated film rather than an ad.

We worked with Willie for a couple of reasons. Mark Crumpacker,
who was our CMO, loved the idea of a newer song and an iconic artist
like Willie Nelson. It became the number two most-downloaded song
on the Apple Music country chart. Willie Nelson is also the founder
of Farm Aid and a huge supporter of family farming, so he ended up
donating the money he got and the royalties to our foundation.

By virtue of having the charity twist, people wanted to be involved
and didn't expect to be paid in the same way they would for a commercial. It wasn't nothing, but in the fast-food category, average spend
on marketing is somewhere in the range of 5 percent to 7 percent of
revenue. We spent 1.5 percent. And the business was performing really
well, so we always had a little bit of a willingness to take chances on
doing things like that. We believed internally in the project, and if
we didn't get much of a return on the investment from a marketing
perspective, it kind of didn't matter, because the results kept coming
anyway. We had a little latitude or luxury that many companies don't
have, just because of our internal realities.

**Was there any concern about telling a sad story? There is a trium-
phant end, but it's also scary at parts and gut-wrenching.**

We liked the strong emotional appeal. We really believed, on issues
of sustainability, that people aren't moved by data. They're moved
by emotion. I deal with this all the time in the dairy industry, where
people just want to club everyone with statistics and climate data. I'm
getting tired of saying, "That's not what breaks through. What gets

people's attention is things that resonate with them emotionally or personally or nostalgically, or some other emotional appeal."

And, at Chipotle, it wasn't a huge leap, because we'd always done these sorts of personal farmer profiles, so basing *Back to the Start* on one guy's story had such authenticity. We had a brand that was so steeped in authenticity that it really felt very true to who we were.

Going back to your first big storytelling moment, the 1993 review, you said, "the now-defunct" paper. The media landscape has really changed since those days. Do you do things differently because of that?

One hundred percent! We became much more reliant on owned media like these short films, things that we could control. We were very smart about doing them in ways where there was emotion or they flirted with controversy in ways that made them very "media-able" also, so they created a lot of earned media.

I was also becoming less enamored of earned media and increasingly concerned about the prospect for blowback. We had become such a media darling, and that kept me awake at night because it can cut both ways. We live in a culture where people seem to love to build up people and institutions and then tear them down. Starbucks is a great example, which in many ways has become a company that people love to hate.

The whole earned media ecosystem was based on clicks. The facts didn't matter. During the food-safety thing [the series of foodborne-illness outbreaks that Chipotle locations experienced starting in 2015], even if there was nothing new in the evolution of that incident for a week, it was still reported every day because people got clicks from it.

It's an interesting era now; there is so much more opportunity for storytelling through owned media. Chipotle was getting more and more into this. We did this "Cultivating Thought" thing where great authors wrote two-hundred-word essays on cups. There's a really funny vignette from Conan O'Brien's show with the author Michael Lewis, who wrote on one of our cups and jokes with Conan that it apparently pays pretty well to write on cups. But it spoke to what kind of affinity people had for Chipotle.

The whole thing came about when Jonathan Safran Foer wrote his book *Eating Animals*. Steve and Mark reached out to him because they were fascinated by his thoughts on the issues around animal agriculture and the ethics of eating animals. Then one day Jonathan was eating in Chipotle, forgot his phone, and was disappointed that there was nothing to read. Later he emailed Steve and said, "You should put stuff on the cups for people like me when they don't have a phone."

Steve, being quick and innovative, said, "That's a great idea. Do you want to do it for us?" So we ended up hiring Jonathan Safran Foer, who wrote one of the cups, but he curated the whole thing. That guy has reach into every literary corner of America, so we had Tina Fey, Sarah Silverman, Toni Morrison, Michael Lewis, Malcolm Gladwell—it was a list of amazing writers and thinkers who would give us two hundred words to put on drink cups. It was all just insane, but we were playing a lot more with that, and I would have continued to move in that direction.

You said that when you are doing well as a company, it almost doesn't matter if your marketing earns financial returns because the company's still marching upward. Then with the food-safety issues, your sales were declining in a way that they never had before. How is storytelling different in a time like that?

That was difficult, in part because the underlying crisis was rooted in the very food that we professed for so long was different and better and special. There was a need to reassure and educate. We had to do a lot of work to talk about what we had done to enhance food safety. We had to embrace some of the more traditional marketing stuff that we didn't do much of before. We became a little bit more promotions-driven, a lot more growth-marketing driven, although we were also really keen to find ways to reclaim our mojo and the things that made us special, akin to what we had done before.

Did that same type of storytelling work again for you?

One of the things that didn't work well and is so sad to me to this day—one of my all-time favorite comms things ever, and it was a big, fizzled dud—was something we called "SAVOR.WAVS." Our marketing had a heavy emphasis on the fact that there were only fifty-one ingredients used to make everything that we served. There're like two and a half times that in a Big Mac alone, because of all the artificial stuff in heavily processed food. We worked with RZA from the Wu-Tang Clan. He wrote little musical stems [isolated audio tracks that can be combined to create a song] for each of the fifty-some ingredients that we had. You could go to our website and click in your Chipotle order, and all those stems associated with those ingredients would then make a song. RZA is a genius. He wrote these things so that you could put them together in any way and they would sound amazing. It was really cool!

We were launching SAVOR.WAVS with an event with RZA and a four-piece band in New York. That day we had a norovirus incident in Virginia, which three years before would have been a non-incident for a single restaurant. But now, anything Chipotle, with any sort of food safety, became national news. Our big thing with RZA totally got crushed by a food-safety fiasco. SAVOR.WAVS was a ploy to get back to talking about the things we wanted to talk about, and just circumstantially it didn't work out.

You mentioned that the *Back to the Start* film was originally conceived for a loyalty program. Tell me more about that sort of storytelling.

We had Burrito Ambassadors, who were part of the early efforts to seed the grassroots word of mouth, and it worked well because people just loved us. They were usually college students, and they did this stuff for basically nothing. We would give them free burrito coupons and swag to share with friends, and because they were such Chipotle fanatics and the brand had so much panache, they were thrilled to do it.

Most of those relationships were born out of frequent customer-service commenters, people who contacted us all the time because they loved us, or through the local store marketing team, who were relatively junior marketing people. We had them in every major market around the country, and their job was basically to help ingrain Chipotle in the fabric of the communities we serve. When we were opening restaurants, they did outreach to major employers and brought free boxes of burritos to employees. We would sponsor neighborhood music festivals or arts festivals, school activities, hyperlocal kinds of things. The Burrito Ambassadors came from those channels, too.

That whole universe of guerrilla marketing and word-of-mouth seeding was born, actually, at the trial of Timothy McVeigh, the Oklahoma City bomber, which was at the federal courthouse in Denver. Our first real activity along those lines was sending boxes of burritos to feed the press corps covering the trial; they said, "Oh, yeah, this was awesome. Not only thanks for the dinner when we can't get away, but I'm going to write about you guys because this is really cool."

When you sent people free burritos, did you also include messaging in the boxes?

No, this was where the ambassadors and the local store marketing team came in. They served the food to, say, the press corps at the Timothy McVeigh trial, and they had been trained to talk about our food and our brand. When we got into the phase later of drawing people in under the auspices of entertainment and whipping a little knowledge on them, we built a series that we called the Cultivate Festivals, that were daylong food, music, and ideas festivals. Great bands would come and play. Celebrity chefs did demos. And we had exhibits contrasting confinement pig farming and a free-ranging pig farm or talking about the promise of GMOs versus the reality of GMOs, and things like that. The exhibits were 100 percent staffed by our people instead of using agency street teams, because our people were able to talk about our brand. We didn't necessarily need to accompany them with written information; it was a much more personal exchange.

Conclusion

I remember the precise moment when my approach to using sustainability as a business driver and a market differentiator became reality, when word of our efforts got beyond the Bon Appétit inner circle and translated into sales. It was 2001—before X (née Twitter). Before YouTube as you know it today. Before Facebook. Before virality in general. We had, quietly, changed our purchasing strategy to boycott the vegetable processor NORPAC, in support of workers' rights. We didn't make any grand pronouncement about this; we just did it.

At the time, our CEO Fedele Bauccio was on the road making sales pitches. At his first stop in Washington, DC, he landed a new account at a school where students had petitioned to oust the current food-service company in favor of us because we had signed on to support farmworkers' rights.

Then, in Ohio, it happened again. Fedele was dumbstruck that this change, which the company had barely mentioned, was landing business for us. So he called me before his next meeting. "Put a brochure together!" he exclaimed. "People care about this stuff!"

Everything you've learned in this book springs from that moment. Fedele's decision to sign on to the cause, born from an emotional connection he felt to the farmworkers, earned us $7 million in new annual revenues. Imagine what would happen when we started telling people about what we were doing.

You can't market manure at lunchtime, but you can drive revenues and create brand loyalty by thoughtfully building sustainability
into your corporate strategy. While your customers may not want to
be burdened with the stinky details, they do increasingly care about
how your product impacts their world. Searches relating to sustainable goods increased by 71 percent globally from 2016 to 2021.[1] Interest
in, and willingness to pay for, ethical practices continues to grow. A
February 2022 survey of 16,000 global consumers by the IBM Institute for Business Value revealed that 51 percent of respondents said
environmental sustainability is more important to them today than
it was just twelve months earlier. They're putting their money where
their values are, with 49 percent of consumers reporting they've paid
a premium—an average of 59 percent more—for products branded as
sustainable or socially responsible in the previous twelve months.[2]

Your business will be rewarded if you *smartly* capitalize on these
market signals. It's not going to be quick or easy though. The road to
sustainability can become the proverbial one to hell if you pave it simply with good intentions. As you've read in my stories and those of
the dozen experts I interviewed, the real work involves focused effort,
hard choices, long-term commitment, systems and operation change,
uncomfortable alliances, and analysis of data until your eyes cross. It
requires new levels of transparency and publicly sharing your journey,
the triumphs *and* the failures. For many, it will be new territory, an
alien environment you're not used to working in. You'll need courage.
But if you can muster it, it will pay off.

Use the early lessons in this book as a to-do list. Pick your battles,
write your mission statement (be it for your company, department, or
yourself), and find the leverage points in your purchasing power and
internal business systems that are the fulcrums to making real change.
Keep the advice on what to do if you fall short in your back pocket
because, unfortunately, at some point you'll experience setbacks.

Then, after all that, put together a brochure, as Fedele urged me to. But
notice we didn't start with the marketing collateral. We accomplished
something first. The brochure comes after some real change, not before.

If you're up to this challenge, you can use the power of the market to change the world. Remember, I'm the logical Mr. Spock in my operation; Fedele's the dreamer. I don't tend toward emotional appeals, but let me say this once more so you know I really mean it:

You can change the world! You can improve the lives of real people in your community and across the globe. You can protect our natural resources. You can set up future generations to have the ability to meet their own needs. You can be proud of what you're leaving the next seven generations. And you can build a profitable business by doing so!

For a long time, I wondered just how those university students had known what we did and had mobilized to force the change that won us business and earned me that breathless call from Fedele to make a brochure. How did the information travel so far so quickly back in 2001?

Two decades later, I was at a dinner with Ramón Ramirez, my fellow board member of the Equitable Food Initiative, who had been the president of the union representing the farmworkers we had signed on to support. We started talking about that boycott and how it was seminal for his organization, and he mentioned that the union had next to no budget and couldn't get the national press interested in farmworkers' rights. So he decided to do a college speaking tour to get the word out.

The tour, he told me, started at a school in Washington, DC, the same one Fedele would visit shortly thereafter. Then he went to Ohio, to the same school Fedele was headed to. This was unplanned, a dumb-luck coincidence. But then again, maybe all that work we put in helped to create that dumb luck. We did the right thing and it paid off.

Your turn now. Do the work, and the universe will reward you.

Notes

Introduction

1. *Our Common Future: Report of the World Commission on Environment and Development*, UN Documents, n.d., http://www.un-documents.net /ocf-02.htm.

2. Indigenous Corporate Training, "What Is the Seventh Generation Principle," May 30, 2020, https://www.ictincca/blog/seventh-generation -principle.

3. United Nations Environment Programme and World Trade Organization, "Making Tourism More Sustainable: A Guide for Policy Makers," 2005, https:// wedocs.unep.org/20.500.11822/8741.

Lesson One

1. Impossible, "About Us," https://impossiblefoods.com/company.

2. Ben & Jerry's, "Our Progressive Values," https://www.benjerry.com /values/our-progressive-values.

3. Tyson, "Farmers," https://www.tysonfoods.com/who-we-are /our-partners/farmers.

Lesson Two

1. Mission Statement Academy, "Chipotle Mission and Vision Statement Analysis," https://mission-statement.com/chipotle/.

2. QDOBA Mexican Eats, "Qdoba Mission, Values & Values," https://www .comparably.com/companies/qdoba/mission.

3. MIXT has updated its website but the original quote can be found under "Why Is MIXT Worth It?" here: https://web.archive.org/web/20190421001954/ https://www.mixt.com/faq/.

4. Sweetgreen, "Our Mission," https://www.sweetgreen.com/mission.

5. Kraft Heinz, "Kraft Heinz Renews Global Commitments in 2020 Environmental Social Governance Report," press release, September 16, 2020, https://news.kraftheinzcompany.com/press-releases-details/2020/Kraft-Heinz -Renews-Global-Commitments-in-2020-Environmental-Social-Governance -Report/default.aspx.

6. "Kraft Heinz Renews Global Commitment in 2020 Environmental Social Governance Report," Business Wire, September 16, 2020, https://www.businesswire.com/news/home/20200916005495/en/Kraft-Heinz-Renews-Global-Commitments-in-2020-Environmental-Social-Governance-Report.

Lesson Three

1. Just Label It!, "About GMO Foods Center," https://www.justlabelit.org/about-ge-foods-center/environmental-impact/.

2. World Wildlife Fund, "Cotton | Overview," https://www.worldwildlife.org/industries/cotton.

3. National Institute of Food and Agriculture, "Family Farms," USDA, https://www.nifa.usda.gov/grants/programs/family-small-farm-program/family-farms.

4. Anil K. Giri et al., "Off-Farm Income a Major Component of Total Income for Most Farm Households in 2019," Economic Research Service, USDA, September 7, 2021, https://www.ers.usda.gov/amber-waves/2021/september/off-farm-income-a-major-component-of-total-income-for-most-farm-households-in-2019/.

5. Lela Nargi, "The University of Kentucky's Long Road to Sourcing 'Local' Food," Civil Eats, February 26, 2019, https://civileats.com/2019/02/26/the-university-of-kentuckys-long-road-to-sourcing-local-food/.

6. Danielle Douglas, "Founding Farmers Restaurant Takes Root in Potomac," *Washington Post*, October 30, 2011, https://www.washingtonpost.com/business/capitalbusiness/founding-farmers-restaurant-takes-root-in-potomac/2011/10/24/gIQAuyw7WM_story.html.

7. Compass Group, "Our Story, CSR 2022," https://issuu.com/compass-pdc/docs/2022_csr; Chipotle, "Cultivate a Better World," *2021 Chipotle Sustainability Report Update*, https://www.chipotle.com/content/dam/chipotle/pages/sustainability/us/2023/updated-2021-annual-cmg-report-update-11-17-22.pdf

8. PepsiCo, "Climate Change," https://www.pepsico.com/our-impact/esg-topics-a-z/climate-change.

9. Sodexo, "Responsible Supply Chain," https://us.sodexo.com/corporate-responsibility/responsible-supply-chain.html.

10. Charlotte Degot et al., "Use AI to Measure Emission—Exhaustively, Accurately, and Frequently," BCG, October 13, 2021, https://www.bcg.com/publications/2021/measuring-emissions-accurately.

11. Chicken Check.In, "What Is the Difference Between Fast- and Slower-Growing Chicken?," National Chicken Council, https://www.chickencheck.in/faq/difference-faster-slower-growing-chicken.

12. Kestrel Burcham, "Slower-Growing Chickens," Cornucopia Institute, March 1, 2018, https://www.cornucopia.org/2018/02/slower-growing-chickens/.

13. McDonald's, "Climate Action," https://corporate.mcdonalds.com/corpmcd/our-purpose-and-impact/our-planet/climate-action.html.

14. Steven H. Foskett Jr., "CEO Appeals for Sustainability," *Telegram & Gazette*, October 5, 2011, https://www.telegram.com/story/news/local/north/2011/10/05/ceo-appeals-for-sustainability/49880406007/.

Interview, Lisa Dyson

1. Good Food Institute, "Record $5 Billion Invested in Alt Proteins in 2021, Surging 60 Percent Since 2020," press release, n.d., https://gfi.org/press/record-5-billion-invested-in-alt-proteins-in-2021/.

Lesson Four

1. "Belcampo Info," Instagram, May 26, 2010, https://www.instagram.com/tv/CPWOV2pHswY/?utm_source=ig_web_copy_link.

2. Elina Shatkin, "Bye Bye, Belcampo. The High-End Meat Company Has Closed Its Doors," LAist, October 19, 2021, https://laist.com/news/food/belcampo-meat-co-high-end-meat-seller-sustainable-butcher-closed-scandal.

3. Elena Kadvany, "The Belcamp Scandal Widens: Once-Popular Meat Company Is Being Investigated by the Feds," *San Francisco Chronicle*, December 7, 2022, https://www.sfchronicle.com/food/article/belcampo-meat-company-17634840.php.

4. Stephanie Breijo, "After Sourcing Scandal, Belcampo Meat Co. Abruptly Closes Stores, Restaurants," *Los Angeles Times*, October 19, 2021, https://www.latimes.com/food/story/2021-10-19/after-a-summer-sourcing-scandal-belcampo-meat-co-abruptly-closes-it.

5. "Butchers Lounge Live," Instagram, July 17, 2022, https://www.instagram.com/tv/CgIvWY8loTN/?igshid=NTc4MTIwNjQ2YQ%3D%3D.

6. Dan Barber, "How I Fell in Love with a Fish," TED Talk, March 10, 2010, https://www.ted.com/talks/dan_barber_how_i_fell_in_love_with_a_fish.

7. Meghan McCarron, "Chef's Fable," Eater, July 6, 2022, https://www.eater.com/22996588/blue-hill-stone-barns-dan-barber-restaurant-work-environment-ingredients.

8. Charles Platkin, Interview with Dan Barber, New York City Food Policy Center, May 11, 2016, nycfoodpolicy.org.

9. McCarron, "Chef's Fable."

10. Honeypatch Squash, Row 7 Seed Company, https://www.row7seeds.com.

11. "Carl Icahn Loses Proxy Fight with McDonald's over Animal Welfare," CNBC, May 26, 2022, https://www.cnbc.com/2022/05/26/carl-icahn-loses-proxy-fight-with-mcdonalds-over-animal-welfare.html.

12. Scott Galloway, "Three Pillars of Crisis Management," X, May 5, 2021, https://twitter.com/profgalloway/status/1390008472985550854?lang=en.

13. Smithfield Foods, "The Group Housing System for Pregnant Sow on Company-Owned Farms at Smithfield Foods," YouTube, https://www.youtube.com/watch?app=desktop&v=lDkadoJgktc.

14. Jonathan Maze, "McDonald's Shuffles Its Executive Team," *Restaurant Business*, June 27, 2022, https://www.restaurantbusinessonline.com/financing/mcdonalds-shuffles-its-executive-team.

Interview, Josh Balk

1. Accountability Board, https://accountabilityboard.org/.

Lesson Five

1. Chipotle Mexican Grill, "2021 Chipotle Sustainability Report Update," Chipotle, 2021, https://www.chipotle.com/content/dam/chipotle/global-site -design/en/documents/sustainability/CHP_2021_SustainabilityReport_ Revised_5-20.pdf.

2. Jayne O'Donnell, "Got a Nasty Fight? Here's Your Man," *USA Today*, July 31, 2006, https://usatoday30.usatoday.com/money/companies/2006-07-31 -lobbyist-usat_x.htm.

3. "43% of Millennials Don't Trust Big Food Companies," Natural Product Insider, November 2, 2015, https://www.naturalproductsinsider.com/claims /43-millennials-dont-trust-big-food-companies.

4. Victoria Petrock, "Gen Z Doesn't Trust Big Business," Insider Intelligence, November 12, 2021, https://www.insiderintelligence.com/content/gen-z-doesnt -trust-big-business.

5. Mark Bittman, "The Future of Cafeteria Food," *New York Times*, May 10, 2011, https://archive.nytimes.com/opinionator.blogs.nytimes.com/2011/05/10 /the-future-of-cafeteria-food/.

6. Patricia Leigh Brown, "A Ballpark Where Yogurt and Fresh Fruit Vie with Tradition," *New York Times*, July 20, 2022, https://www.nytimes.com /2002/07/20/us/a-ballpark-where-yogurt-and-fresh-fruit-vie-with-tradition .html?searchResultPosition=1.

7. Andrew Evers and Deborah Findling, "The Companies with the Most Impressive Free Food in Silicon Valley," CNBC, May 31, 2018, https://www.cnbc .com/2018/05/30/which-tech-company-has-the-best-free-food.html.

8. "When Do Sustainability Advocates Become Eco-Nazis?," *SF Weekly*, September 1, 2010, https://www.sfweekly.com/dining/when-do-sustainabilty -advocates-become-eco-nazis/article_def4151a-08a7-5ff6-a9cd-873b8dd53ddc .html.

9. Maisie Ganzler, "Dear Big Ag: Stop Treating Customers Like They're Stupid," *Des Moines Register*, July 13, 2015, https://www.desmoinesregister .com/story/opinion/columnists/2015/07/14/big-ag-treat-customers-like -stupid/30120787/.

10. Deena Shanker, Leslie Patton, and Michael Hirtzer, "Big Pork Producers Just Can't Quit Gestation Crates," Bloomberg, February 15, 2023, https://www .bloomberg.com/news/articles/2023-02-15/pork-prices-are-a-key-issue-in -debate-over-gestation-crates.

Interview, Chris Arnold

1. Eric Asimov, "$25 and Under; When There's Only One of a Chain," *New York Times*, September 17, 2003, https://www.nytimes.com/2003/09/17/dining /25-and-under-when-there-s-only-one-of-a-chain.html?searchResultPosition=5.

Conclusion

1. "The Eco-Wakening," WWF, n.d., https://explore.panda.org/eco -wakening.

2. Jane Cheung et al., "Balancing Sustainability and Profitability," IBM Institute for Business Value, April 7, 2022, https://www.ibm.com/thought -leadership/institute-business-value/en-us/report/2022-sustainability -consumer-research.

Index

Acknowledgments

Thank you to my parents, Arline and Henry Ganzler, who took me to travel the world at an early age, opening my eyes to both the diversity and universality of people. They modeled being active members of their communities and working for the good of others, and they clearly informed my take on success.

Fedele Bauccio has played a pivotal role in my life. I would be a different leader, thinker, and person had I not met him, and I surely wouldn't have had these lessons to share. I'm equally indebted to the quirky, caring people of Bon Appétit Management Company. The advice in this book is tried and tested because they put my ideas into action in real-life operations and challenged me when my theories weren't practical. They worked out the kinks and created the true magic. Working with Fedele and this extraordinary team has been one of my life's greatest blessings. I'm incredibly proud of all we've accomplished together.

Corey Ridings was the first person to suggest I knew something worthy of a book. Having someone that smart believe in the value of my perspective was the confidence boost I needed to start. Then James White, a fairy godfather of sorts, introduced me to Scott Berinato at Harvard Business Review Press. Scott always had a surprising analogy and insightful edit at the ready. He and the world-class team at the Press made the path to publication surprisingly easy.

Devin Fuller kept me from writing in a vacuum. She let me talk out my thoughts when the words weren't flowing to the page, found structure in my stories, and acted as my first audience. As we passed documents back and forth, I eagerly looked forward to reading her track changes and comments, and I mentally rejoiced when I got a written indication of laughter. Writing this book would've been very lonely without her.

Twelve exceptionally busy people generously agreed to share their wisdom: Chris Arnold, Josh Balk, Fedele Bauccio, Lisa Dyson, Ernie Farley, Gary Hirshberg, David Kinch, Roma McCaig, Rob Michalak, Jim Perdue, Walter Robb, and Shauna Sadowski. Their openness, generosity, and willingness to talk about their successes and stumbles consistently wowed me. I learned a great deal from our conversations and am excited for others to benefit from their experience.

Early readers provided both critical feedback and encouragement: Bonnie Azab Powell, Jeff Bareilles, Pooja Bhatia, Adam Brumberg, Nicole Tocco Cardwell, Megan Farley, Olivia Fisher, Renee Guilbault, Andrea Nguyen, Corey Ridings, and Shally Shanker. They were my reality check in multiple ways, and I deeply appreciate them giving me their precious time.

And I'm filled with love and gratitude for David, who helped me reimagine the next phase of my life after the original picture was blurred, and with whom I hope to travel the world, laughing, eating, and doing puzzles, into old age.

About the Author

MAISIE GANZLER is a straight-talking businesswoman, an activist, and a renowned expert on branding and sustainability. As chief strategy and brand officer, she helped Bon Appétit Management Company grow to almost $2 billion by simultaneously driving food systems change and corporate profitability.

Her perspective is frequently sought out by leading media outlets, including the *New York Times*, *Wall Street Journal*, NPR, *Fast Company*, and *Bloomberg*. She has been published as a contributing columnist in the *Huffington Post* and *Forbes*, and she is regularly tapped by venture capitalists to give strategic advice to startups.

Maisie splits her time between Santa Cruz, CA, Puerto Vallarta, Mexico, and anywhere else in the world she's given the opportunity to explore.